A.

if found please call...
- 630 281 4104
- 860 977 9222

Kailasanathar Temple, Ellora
carved into the rock face of Charanandri Hills in the eighth century

Indus Valley
2,500 bce

Saint Tiruvalluvar
200 bce

Mahatma Gandhi
1869-1948

Diwaii, the Festival of Light
2010

SOCIAL STUDIES

The History of
HINDU INDIA

From Ancient to Modern Times

**Editors of
HINDUISM TODAY
Magazine**

Dr. Shiva Bajpai

HIMALAYAN ACADEMY PUBLICATIONS
INDIA/USA

Authors

THE EDITORS OF HINDUISM TODAY MAGAZINE

HINDUISM TODAY magazine was founded in 1979 to inform and educate Hindus and non-Hindus alike about Hinduism. The material in this book was created over a period of four years in collaboration with Dr. Shiva Bajpai. It has been reviewed by a panel of academic experts and Hindu community consultants. In addition to *HINDUISM TODAY*, Himalayan Academy publishes numerous books, including *What Is Hinduism?, Loving Ganesha, How to Become a Hindu, Weaver's Wisdom,* and the series *Dancing with Siva, Living with Siva* and *Merging with Siva.* It also publishes educational materials and storybooks for children.

DR. SHIVA BAJPAI

Dr. Shiva G. Bajpai served as Professor of History and Director of Asian Studies at California State University, Northridge, Los Angeles, from 1970 to 2003. As Professor Emeritus, he continued to teach from 2003 to 2009. He has BA and MA from Banares Hindu University and a Ph.D. from the School of Oriental and African Studies, University of London, UK. He has published numerous articles on Indian history and culture, and he co-authored the major reference work *A Historical Atlas of South Asia.* He served as a content review panel expert during the 2005 California adoption process for sixth-grade social studies textbooks.

First Edition
Copyright © 2011 Himalayan Academy
The History of Hindu India is published by Himalayan Academy. All rights are reserved. This book may be reproduced only with the publisher's prior written consent. Designed, typeset and illustrated by the editorial staff of Himalayan Academy, publishers of *HINDUISM TODAY* magazine, 107 Kaholalele Road, Kapaa, Hawaii 96746-9304 USA. Also available in various eBook formats at himalayanacademy.com/history/

Published by
Himalayan Academy
India • USA

PRINTED IN USA

Library of Congress Control Number: 2011938171
ISBN 978-1-934145-38-8 (hardcover)
ISBN 978-1-934145-41-8 (eBook)

Academic Reviewers

Dr. Klaus Klostermaier
Professor of Religious Studies
University of Manitoba
Winnipeg, Manitoba

Dr. Jeffrey D. Long
Chair, Department of Religious Studies
Elizabethtown College
Elizabethtown, Pennsylvania

Dr. Anantanand Rambachan
Professor of Religion
St. Olaf College
Northfield, Minnesota

Dr. T.S. Rukmani (chapters 1 through 4)
Professor and Chair in Hindu Studies
Concordia University
Montreal, Quebec

Dr. Michael K. Ward
Visiting Lecturer in History
California State University
Northridge, California

Community Consultants

Dr. Ved P. Chaudhary
President, Educators' Society for the
Heritage of India (ESHI)
Morganville, New Jersey

Suhag A. Shukla, Esq.
Co-Founder/Managing Director
Hindu American Foundation
Washington, DC

Educational Reviewer

Justin Stein, M.A., Ph.D. student
Former New York middle school teacher
University of Toronto, Ontario

Contents

CHAPTER 6

Hindu Festivals

RESOURCES

Hinduism From Ancient Times

This young priest is conducting a fire ceremony just as was done in ancient times.

What You Will Learn...

The largest civilization in the ancient world developed in the Indus Valley of India over 5,000 years ago. In the thousands of years that followed, India produced many great empires under which science, art and philosophy flourished. Out of this rich history developed the Hindu religion, today the third largest in the world.

Origins of Hinduism

What You Will Learn...

Main Ideas

1. Many Hindu religious practices are seen in the archeological remains of the Indus-Sarasvati civilization.
2. The sacred texts of Hinduism are in the Sanskrit language and were originally memorized but unwritten.
3. Ancient Indian art and science were highly developed.

The Big Idea

Hinduism developed over thousands of years in India.

Key Terms

Indus and Sarasvati rivers, p. 2; *Vedas*, p. 3; Sanskrit, p. 3

HINDUISM TODAY'S TEACHING STANDARDS

This column in each section presents our outline for teaching Hinduism in 6th grade social studies.

1. Explain the similarities between Indus-Sarasvati civilization and later Hindu culture.
2. Discuss why the Aryan Invasion theory has been disputed by many scholars.
3. Discuss the social and political system and advancement of science and culture.
4. Explain the development of religion in India between 1000 bce and 500 ce.

If YOU lived then...

Your house is built on a wide, waterless riverbed. Your father tells you it was once the giant Sarasvati River, five kilometers across. There is not enough rain to provide for the family's crops and cattle. Travelers tell of another great river, the Ganga, hundreds of miles away. Your father and other villagers decide they must move.

How would you feel about the long journey?

BUILDING BACKGROUND India's known history begins with the Indus-Sarasvati civilization, 5,500 years ago. We know from archeology that this culture shows many features of later Hindu practice.

Understanding Ancient Indian History

The early cities of India developed along the Indus and Sarasvati rivers starting around 3500 bce. They are called the Indus-Sarasvati civilization or, sometimes, the Harappan culture. It was the largest and most advanced civilization in the ancient world. But the mighty Sarasvati River dried up, and what was once a fertile area became a desert. The people of the region moved to other parts of India and beyond. By 2000 bce the civilization had entered a period of decline.

The Religion of the Indus-Sarasvati People

A great many artifacts have been discovered from the Indus-Sarasvati cities. These include pottery, seals, statues, beads, jewelry, tools, games, such as dice, and children's toys, such as miniature carts.

The flat, stone seals have pictures and writing on them. Scholars have not yet agreed on what the mysterious script on the seals means. They show deities, ceremonies, symbols, people, plants and animals. We learn from them that people at that time followed practices identical to those followed by Hindus today. One seal shows a meditating figure that scholars link to Lord Siva, while others show the lotus posture used by today's meditators. The swastika, a sacred symbol of good luck used throughout Hindu history, is common.

There are statues, including a small clay figure with its hands pressed together in the traditional Hindu greeting of "namaste."

A figurine of a married woman shows a red powder called *sindur* in the part of her hair. Hindu women today follow this same custom as a sign of their married status. The pipal tree and banyan tree are depicted often. These remain sacred to Hindus to this day.

The *Vedas*

The central holy books of Hinduism are the four *Vedas*. Hindus regard them as spoken by God. They are in Sanskrit. The *Vedas* were not written down but memorized. Students might spend twelve years learning these scriptures. Some would memorize one *Veda*, others all four. Even today there are priests who can chant an entire *Veda*—as many as 10,500 verses—from memory.

The relationship between the people of the Indus-Sarasvati civilization and those who composed the *Vedas* is not clearly understood. We know that the *Rig Veda* describes the Sarasvati as the "most mighty of rivers" flowing from the Himalayan mountains to the ocean. Therefore, the holy texts had to be composed well before 2000 bce—by which time the river had dried up. The *Vedas* describe a powerful and spiritual people, their clans, kings and emperors. Their society was complex. The economy included agriculture, industry, trade, commerce and cattle raising. The *Vedas* contain thousands of hymns in praise of God and the Gods. They describe a form of fire worship, yajna, around a specially-built brick fire altar. In several Indus-Sarasvati cities archeologists have unearthed what look like fire altars.

The Aryan Invasion Theory

Many school books present an "Aryan Invasion" of India. It is the theory that Aryan invaders came from central Asia in 1500 bce and conquered the indigenous Indus-Sarasvati civilization. It was these foreigners, the theory states, who wrote the *Rig Veda* in Sanskrit. The theory was proposed in the 19th century by scholars in Europe,

HINDU SYMBOLS

The banyan tree is a symbol of Hinduism because it gives shelter to all who approach

THE IMPACT Today

The disputed Aryan Invasion theory is still taught as fact in most books on India

FROM INDUS-SARASVATI TO MODERN TIMES

Indus-Sarasvati sculptures, seals and artifacts more than 5,000 years old display features of modern Hinduism

Lord Siva in meditation is found on the Indus seals

At left is a clay figure showing the typical Hindu greeting of "namaste"

This clay figure of a woman has red *sindur* in the hair part—a custom followed by married Hindu women to this day

based on language studies. In part, it tried to explain why Sanskrit is so closely related to European languages, including English. Many scholars now dispute this theory because all the evidence for it is questionable. Additionally, modern scientists have found no biological evidence, such as DNA, that people came from outside India in significant numbers since at least 6,000 bce.

Many common explanations about Indian history and culture are based on the Aryan Invasion theory. Those who defend it claim that Sanskrit, the caste system and Hindu ways of worship came from outside India. If you are studying India in school, you may read about this outdated theory.

Hinduism Emerges

As the Indus-Sarasvati culture declined, many of its people migrated to other places. They settled mostly in north and central India, especially along the Ganga River system. They interacted with tribes who had lived in those areas from ancient times. Around 1000 bce, the Tamil-speaking Dravidian people in the South had separately developed a sophisticated language and

culture. Because of inadequate archeological research, we do not know a lot about this period. However, by 600 bce, India had developed a common culture from north to south and east to west. By this time the social, religious and philosophical ideas and practices central to Hinduism are fully evident. These are in **continuity** with the religion of the Indus-Sarasvati culture, the teachings of the *Vedas,* Dravidian culture and elements of the tribal religions.

Hindu public worship, described in the *Vedas,* took place in temporary shelters built for that purpose. The earliest mention of permanent temples for the worship of God is in the *Grihya Sutras,* around 600 bce.

Indian Society

A distinctive feature of India at this time was the varna or class system. Society was classified into groups with specific occupations. These groups tended to become **hereditary**. There were four broad classes—priests, warriors, merchants and workers (including craftsmen). The system provided order and stability to society. Later on, the varnas divided into hundreds of sub-sections called *jatis* (castes). Individual *jatis* developed a

Timeline: Early Indian History

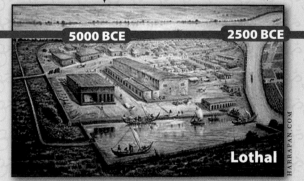

5000 BCE
Beginning of Indus-Sarasvati cities

2600-2000 BCE
Height of Indus-Sarasvati civilization. The city of Lothal includes large buildings and an enclosed harbor.

5000 BCE   **2500 BCE**   **1000 BCE**

Lothal

2000 BCE
Sarasvati River dries up. People move to North and Central India.

600 BCE
India is a unified culture at this time. Large cities flourish in the Gangetic Plains. Indian physician Sushruta develops complex methods of surgery. Tamil language flourishes in the South. First mention of temple worship appears in the *Grihya Sutras.*

strong identity and pride in their occupation. From time to time people would move from one caste to another, or establish new ones. The evolving caste system became unfair to the people at the very bottom of the social order. Though caste is still an important factor in arranging marriages, caste discrimination is illegal in modern India.

Women have always been held in high regard in India. Some of India's foremost religious and political leaders are women. Hinduism is the only major religion in which God is worshiped in female form.

Life in ancient times was hard work for both men and women. The women were responsible for running the household; the men for their craft or farm, as well as security. In general, women had fewer property rights than men, but received lighter punishments for crimes and paid fewer taxes. They participated equally with their husband in religious ceremonies and festival celebrations. Some women were highly educated, and a few even composed several of the holy Vedic hymns.

The period from 1000 bce through the Gupta period up to the mid-6th century ce was a time of great advancement. Hindus discovered the zero and established the counting method, including the decimal system, we use today. Their astronomers knew that the Earth orbits the Sun and calculated the length of a year with great precision.

Medicine was so advanced that doctors were performing complex surgery not equaled in Europe until the 18th century. In ancient times India was one of the most advanced and wealthy nations on Earth. Since ancient times, a quarter of the world's people have lived in India.

Section 1 Assessment

REVIEWING IDEAS, TERMS AND PEOPLE

1. a. **Explain** What happened to the Sarasvati River?
   b. **Analyze** What customs from modern Hinduism are depicted in artifacts of the Indus-Sarasvati civilization?
2. **Elaborate** What are the advantages of a hereditary occupation? What are the disadvantages?
3. a. **Summarize** How are women regarded in Hindu society?
   b. **Recall** What are some of the great scientific achievements in ancient India?
4. a. **Explain** How were the *Vedas* preserved?
   b. **List** What kind of information is in the *Vedas?*
   c. **Explain** Why is it important that the Rig Veda mentions the Sarasvati River as a "mighty river?"

FOCUS ON WRITING

5. **Analyze** What does your school history book say about the Aryan Invasion? How does this lesson differ?

Sushruta

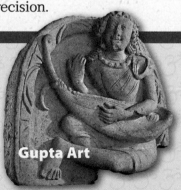
Gupta Art

Angkor Wat 1200 ce

321 BCE
Foundation of the pan-Indian Maurya Empire. Time of great advancement in science, statecraft, economy, architecture, music and art.

200 CE
Hindu influence starts to spread into what is now Cambodia, Thailand, Malaysia and Indonesia. In 1200 ce, the Hindu temple called Angkor Wat is built in Cambodia. It is the world's largest religious structure.

500 BCE | 200 BCE | 300 CE

500 BCE
Magadha Empire in the North and Pandyan Kingdom in the South flourish. Buddhism and Jainism, offshoots of Hinduism, become prominent religions.

200 BCE
Tiruvalluvar composes *Tirukural*, one of India's greatest scriptures on ethics

S. RAJAM

320 CE
Gupta Empire reigns over most of India, with Tamil kingdoms in far south. This is the Golden Age of India and Hinduism, with respect and tolerance for all religions.

Hindu Beliefs and Scriptures

If YOU lived then...

The king has passed a new law increasing the taxes on farmers. The farmers in your village have not had a good year. The harvest is smaller than usual. The new tax may mean people will go hungry. Some in the village want to attack the tax collectors. Others want to lie about the amount of harvest. Still others say a peaceful protest will cause the king to change his mind on the tax increase.

How would you respond to the tax increase? Why?

BUILDING BACKGROUND From its beginnings, Hinduism has been an open-minded religion. It is a basic Hindu belief that there are many ways to approach God. Hinduism does not dictate one way as the only way. Hindus believe "Truth is one, paths are many" and that every person eventually finds spiritual salvation.

Religion Permeates the Hindu's Daily Life

Hindus base their way of life upon their religion. The Hindu culture comes from Hindu beliefs. The key beliefs are in a one Supreme God, **subordinate** Gods and Goddesses, heaven worlds, the divinity of the soul, dharma, karma, reincarnation, God Realization and liberation from rebirth. God Realization means the direct and personal experience of the Divine within oneself. The original Sanskrit name for Hinduism is *Sanatana Dharma*, meaning "eternal religion."

Belief in God and the Gods and Goddesses

Hindus believe in and worship a one Supreme God. In the scriptures, the Supreme God is called Brahman or Bhagavan, worshiped as both male and female. Brahman is all-powerful, all-knowing, all-loving and present in all things. God created everything in the universe out of Himself. This creation is not separate from Him. He guides the evolution of everything over vast spans of time. Ultimately, He absorbs the universe back into Himself. This cycle of creation, preservation and absorption repeats without end.

The Supreme God is both transcendent and immanent. These are two key philosophical concepts. As *transcendent*, God exists beyond the physical universe. As *immanent*, His divine form **pervades** all nature and humanity.

In Hinduism, the soul is called atman. God exists within each soul. The *Chandogya Upanishad* explains it like this: "What you see when you look into another person's eyes, that is atman, immortal, beyond fear; that is God."

Hinduism has different branches with varying beliefs and practices. The four major branches are Saiva, Shakta, Vaishnava and Smarta. Saivas and Shaktas call the Supreme God Siva, though Shaktas worship the female aspect of God. Vaishnavas call Him Vishnu. Smartas may choose one of six Deities to worship as the Supreme. By whichever name or form, He is the same, one Supreme God. The *Rig Veda* says, "The seers call in many ways that which is One."

Hindus may also worship Gods and Goddesses, called devas, such as Ganesha and Sarasvati. In Sanskrit, *deva* means "shining one." In some ways, these divine beings who live in the heaven worlds are like the angels and archangels in Western religions. Some Hindus consider the Gods and Goddesses as alternative forms of the Supreme God, and not as individual divine beings.

Each God and Goddess has particular powers and areas of responsibility. For example, Ganesha is the Lord of Obstacles. Before beginning a new project, a Hindu may pray to Ganesha to remove any obstacles blocking his way.

In the Vaishnava tradition, Lord Vishnu appears on Earth as a divine personality, or avatar, from time to time to restore morally right living. Of Vishnu's ten avatars, Lord Rama and Lord Krishna are the most important. Rama and Krishna are not separate Gods. They are two forms of the one Supreme God.

In temples and shrines, the Supreme God and the Gods and Goddesses are worshiped in a ritual called puja. Puja is a ceremony in which the ringing of bells, passing of flames, chanting and presenting of flowers, incense and other offerings

A *kalasha* is a husked coconut set in a brass pot with mango leaves. It is used in worship to represent the Supreme God or any of the Gods or Goddesses.

ACADEMIC VOCABULARY

subordinate lower in rank, less important

pervade to be present throughout

encompass to surround and hold within

ONE SUPREME GOD AND MANY GODS AND GODDESSES

Hindus believe in a one supreme and loving God. At the same time, they believe in Gods and Goddesses, great spiritual beings who help us.

ALL ART: INDRA SHARMA

Ganesha is the God prayed to before beginning any task or worship. His elephant head makes Him easy to recognize.

Sarasvati is the Goddess of learning and music. Below, She sits on a lotus flower playing the multi-stringed vina.

In the *Bhagavad Gita* Lord Krishna shows Arjuna His universal form as the Supreme God encompassing all the other Gods

NONVIOLENCE

The Hindu principle of ahimsa, or nonviolence, is important today. Mahatma Gandhi, a devout Hindu, said, "Nonviolence is the greatest force at the disposal of mankind. It is mightier than the mightiest weapon of destruction devised by the ingenuity of man." By nonviolent means Gandhi largely won India's independence, using peaceful protests, boycotts, strikes and speeches. In the 1950s, Martin Luther King, Jr. studied Gandhi's methods and went to India to meet his followers. He learned how India's nonviolent movement worked and applied the same methods to fight for and win civil rights for America's black minority. Aung San Suu Kyi, a devout Buddhist, has campaigned without violence for years to win democracy for the people of her native Myanmar (Burma). In 1991 she won the Nobel Peace Prize for her peaceful struggle against the country's military dictatorship. Another example is Cesar Chavez, who won rights for California farm workers using nonviolent methods.

ANALYSIS
SKILL **ANALYZING INFORMATION**

What are the advantages of nonviolence over violence in bringing about social change?

BLACKSTAR PHOTOS/FLIP SCHULKE

DINODIA

REUTERS/APICHART WEERAWONG

ACADEMIC VOCABULARY

consecrated
made sacred through ceremony

invoke
summon a Deity; appeal to

HINDU SYMBOLS

The orange or red banner is the flag of Hinduism, which flies above temples, at festivals and in parades

invoke the Divine beings, who then come to bless and help the devotees. During the puja, through holy chants, gestures and sacred ritual, highly trained priests guide the worship. The priests treat the Deity with utmost care, attending to Him as the King of kings. The purpose of the puja is to create a high religious vibration and communicate with God or a deva through the *murti*, or **consecrated** statue, that is the focus of worship. *Deity* is the proper English word for *murti*. The word *idol* is often used, but it is incorrect.

Hindus also practice internal worship of God. Sitting quietly, they may repeat the name of God while counting on beads. Others may chant, sing or meditate upon God. In Hinduism, there are many ways to worship the Divine.

Dharma, Karma and Reincarnation

Dharma means righteousness, divine law, ethics, religion, duty, justice and truth. Dharma means the proper way one should live one's life. To follow dharma, one should be religious, truthful, kind, honest and generous. Dharma includes the practice of nonviolence, called ahimsa in Sanskrit. It is the ideal of not injuring others in thought, word or action.

Karma, a central Hindu belief, is the law of cause and effect. It means that anything you do will eventually return to you in this or future lives. If we do something selfish or hateful, we will in time experience the same pain and suffering we caused to others. If our acts are good and kind, we will receive goodness and kindness.

Reincarnation means literally to "re-enter the flesh." It is the belief that the soul, atman, is reborn in a new body, experiencing many lifetimes. The purpose of rebirth is to progressively achieve spiritual maturity and God Realization. Eventually each soul learns to live by religious principles and avoid creating negative karma. The process of reincarnation continues through many lives until the soul achieves liberation.

Hinduism's Sacred Scriptures

The four *Vedas* are the holiest scriptures for all Hindus. The *Upanishads*, an important part of the *Vedas*, explain the Hindu philosophy. The next most important scriptures, also in Sanskrit, are the *Agamas*. There are specific *Agamas* for each major tradition in Hinduism—Saiva, Shakta and Vaishnava. The *Agamas* explain philosophy, personal conduct, worship and temple construction. There are hundreds of other scriptural texts dealing with religious and **secular** law, government, social order, economics, ecology, health, architecture, science, music, astronomy and many other subjects. The *Puranas* are encyclopedic accounts of the forms and avatars of God, the many subordinate Gods and divine beings, creation, spiritual teachings, historical traditions, geography and culture. The *Tirukural* is a Tamil masterpiece on ethics and moral living. The *Yoga Sutras* of Patan-jali explore yoga and meditation.

The *Ramayana* and *Mahabharata* are two sacred epic histories of India. The *Ramayana* is the story of Lord Rama, who is the seventh incarnation of Lord Vishnu, and his divine wife Sita. This 24,000-verse poem describes Prince Rama's birth, His banishment to a forest for 14 years, the abduction of Sita by the demon Ravana and Rama's victory over Ravana. The *Ramayana* remains immensely popular to this day in India and Southeast Asia.

The *Mahabharata,* "Great India," is a 78,000-verse story of a massive war that took place in ancient times between the Pandavas and their cousins, the Kauravas, for the throne of a great kingdom. It also describes the nature of self and the world, karma, important family lineages of India, human loyalties, saints and sages, devotion to God and the ideals of dharma. Lord Krishna, the eighth incarnation of Lord Vishnu, is a key figure in the epic. A central episode called the *Bhagavad Gita* narrates Krishna's dialogue with the Pandava archer, Arjuna, on the day of the battle. It is one of the most popular and revered among Vaishnava and Smarta scriptures. Hindu sacred music, dance, drama and the arts draw heavily on the *Ramayana*, the *Mahabharata* and the many *Puranas*.

Section 2 Assessment

REVIEWING IDEAS, TERMS AND PEOPLE

1. a. **Define** What is Sanatana Dharma?
   b. **Explain** What is a deva?
   c. **Elaborate** What are the two key terms used by Hindus to describe the Supreme God?
2. **Categorize** What are the four main branches of Hinduism?
3. a. **Recall** Why do Hindus pray first to Lord Ganesha?
   b. **Identify** What are the two most popular incarnations of Lord Vishnu?
   c. **Explain** What is the purpose of the Hindu puja?
4. a. **Explain** What is karma?
   b. **Illustrate** What are some examples of following dharma?
   c. **Explain** What is the purpose of reincarnation?

5. **Summarize** Make a list of Hindu scriptures, starting with the *Vedas*.

CRITICAL THINKING

6. **Evaluate** Why do Hindus believe that there are many ways to approach the Supreme God?

FOCUS ON WRITING

7. **Understanding nonviolence**
   Write a paragraph explaining your way to deal with the tax increase example given on page six. Do you think a nonviolent approach would succeed?

The sacred sound *aum* is chanted at the beginning and end of most prayers

GUIDED READING

Word Help

philosophy
a theory or attitude that guides behavior

vain
excessively proud

mysterious
unknown

consume
to destroy completely, as by fire

❶ This verse says that the Gods were vain.
What test did the Supreme God put them through?

from the

Upanishads

Translated by Swami Prabhavananda and Frederick Manchester

The *Upanishads* are the part of the *Vedas* that teach **philosophy**. The word *upanishad* means "sitting by devotedly," as a student sits near his guru to learn. This excerpt is taken from the *Kena Upanishad*. It explains the nature of the Supreme God, called *Brahman* in Sanskrit.

AS YOU READ Try to sum up the meaning of each sentence in your own words.

Once the Gods won a victory over the demons, and though they had done so only through the power of Brahman, they were exceedingly **vain**. They thought to themselves, "It was we who beat our enemies, and the glory is ours."

Brahman saw their vanity and appeared before them as a nature spirit. But they did not recognize Him. ❶

Then the other Gods said to the God of fire, "Fire, find out for us who this **mysterious** nature spirit is."

"Yes," said the God of fire, and approached the spirit. The spirit said to him: "Who are you?"

"I am the God of fire. As a matter of fact, I am very widely known."

"And what power do you wield?"

"I can burn anything on Earth."

"Burn this," said the spirit, placing a straw before him. The God of fire fell upon it with all his might, but could not **consume** it. So he ran back to the other Gods and said, "I cannot discover who this mysterious spirit is."

Then said the other Gods to the God of wind: "Wind, can you find out for us who he is?"

"Yes," said the God of wind, and approached the spirit. The

The *Vedas* and *Upanishads* are written in Sanskrit, a language that is thousands of years old

spirit said to him: "Who are you?"

"I am the God of wind. As a matter of fact, I am very widely known. I fly swiftly through the heavens."

"And what power do you wield?"

"I can blow away anything on Earth."

"Blow this away," said the spirit, placing a straw before him. The God of wind fell upon it with all his might, but was unable to move it. So he ran back to the other Gods and said, "I cannot discover who this mysterious spirit is."

Then said the other Gods to Indra, greatest of them all, "O respected one, find out for us, we pray you, who he is."

"Yes," said Indra and humbly approached the spirit. But the ❷ spirit vanished, and in his place stood Goddess Uma, well **adorned** and of exceeding beauty. **Beholding** her, Indra asked:

"Who was the spirit that appeared to us?"

"That," answered Uma, "was Brahman. Through Him it was, not of yourselves, that you **attained** your victory and your glory."

Thus did Indra, and the God of fire, and the God of wind, come to recognize Brahman, the Supreme God.

GUIDED READING

Word Help

adorned
beautifully dressed

beholding
looking at something remarkable

attained
won; achieved

❷ Indra took a different approach to finding out who the spirit was. *Why did he succeed when the others failed?*

Understanding Sacred Texts

1. **Analyzing** Hindus believe that the Supreme God is *immanent*. That means He exists everywhere in the universe, in everyone and everything. How does this belief appear in the story?

2. **Comparing** What is the difference between Brahman, the Supreme God, and the other Gods introduced here—Indra, the God of fire and the God of wind?

Hinduism in Practice

What You Will Learn...

Main Ideas

1. Hinduism has spread outside of India several times.
2. Hinduism is the third largest religion in the world.
3. Hindus practice religion at home and in temples and through the many festivals.

The Big Idea

Hinduism is the oldest world religion flourishing today.

Key Terms

samskara, *p. 12*
bindi, *p. 12*
puja, *p. 13*
swami, *p. 14*
Kumbha Mela, *p. 15*

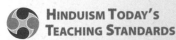

HINDUISM TODAY'S TEACHING STANDARDS

8. Describe the spread of Hinduism outside of India in ancient and modern times.
9. Describe the daily observances of Hindus, home and temple worship, religious teachers and the major festivals.
10. Explain how Hinduism has survived over the last 5,000 years.

If **YOU** lived then...

You are born in Fiji in 1910. Your parents were brought from India by the British to work in the sugarcane fields as **indentured** laborers. Now they are free of debt and own farmland. The public school is OK, but your parents want you to go to the best private school. The principal there says you must leave Hinduism and convert to his religion before you can enroll.

What do you think your parents would do?

BUILDING BACKGROUND Hinduism is the only major religion from the distant past that is still vibrant today. It survived because of its tradition of home-centered worship, because of its rich teachings and many religious leaders, and because it is not merely tolerant of other religions but respects the validity of all spiritual paths.

Traditions and Holy Days

Hinduism is the oldest living religion in the world. There are today nearly a billion Hindus worldwide, 95 percent of whom live on the Indian subcontinent. Hinduism continues to thrive for many reasons. Its followers find answers to their deepest questions about the mysteries of life. With personal religious practices, pilgrimage to sacred shrines, temple- and home-centered worship, Hindus strive for God Realization. And through celebration of the yearly cycle of vibrant and colorful festivals, they experience great blessings and joy.

Basic Practices

There are five basic practices, *pancha nitya karmas*, often observed by Hindus. They are to: 1) worship daily, 2) follow dharma, 3) observe the samskaras (rites of passage), 4) celebrate the holy days and 5) go on pilgrimage to sacred places. Other practices include meditation, chanting of mantras, study of scripture, hatha yoga and other yoga techniques, and simple **austerities**, such as fasting. There are many samskaras, including a child's name-giving ceremony, the first feeding of solid food, the beginning of formal education and marriage. It is a common practice for Hindu women to wear a bindi, a red dot on the forehead. A similar mark, called *tilaka*, is worn by

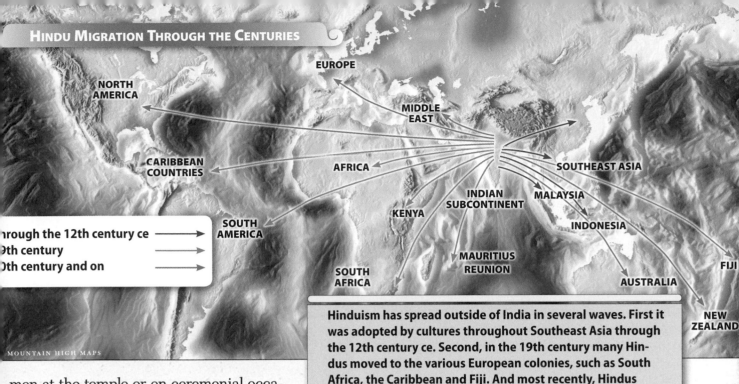

EUROPE

NORTH AMERICA

MIDDLE EAST

CARIBBEAN COUNTRIES

AFRICA

SOUTHEAST ASIA

INDIAN SUBCONTINENT

MALAYSIA

KENYA

SOUTH AMERICA

INDONESIA

hrough the 12th century ce
9th century
0th century and on

FIJI

MAURITIUS REUNION

SOUTH AFRICA

AUSTRALIA

NEW ZEALAND

MOUNTAIN HIGH MAPS

Hinduism has spread outside of India in several waves. First it was adopted by cultures throughout Southeast Asia through the 12th century ce. Second, in the 19th century many Hindus moved to the various European colonies, such as South Africa, the Caribbean and Fiji. And most recently, Hindus migrated to more than 150 countries in the 20th century.

men at the temple or on ceremonial occasions. This forehead mark symbolizes many things, especially spiritual vision.

Worship in the Home

Every Hindu home has a place of worship. It may be as simple as a shelf with pictures of God or an entire room dedicated to worship. Many families have a spiritual guide or guru whose picture is displayed in the shrine. There, the family may light a lamp, ring a bell and pray daily. The most devout hold a formal morning worship ritual. They offer flowers, incense, lights and food to God while chanting sacred verses. Individual members will often go to the shrine for blessings before leaving for school or work. At other times one may sit alone in the shrine, pray and chant the names of God, read from scripture, **meditate** silently or sing devotional songs.

Temple Worship

Hindus prefer to live within a day's journey of a temple. The temple is a special building, revered as the home of God. The main Deity is enshrined in the temple's central sanctum. In India, there are hundreds of thousands of temples, most quite ancient. Temples in India can be enormous, covering many acres, having vast pillared hallways that can accommodate 500,000 devotees during a festival. Often one or more families of priests oversee the temple and conduct the worship over many generations. When Hindus migrate outside India, they build a temple as soon as possible. At first, community leaders themselves conduct the daily rituals. Later, professional priests are hired. There are now hundreds of Hindu temples in America. The largest are in New York, Pennsylvania, Illinois, Texas and California.

The temple worship ceremony, or puja, is usually performed by a priest from India. During the ceremony, he worships God by chanting Sanskrit verses from the scriptures and performing *arati*. *Arati* is the waving of an oil lamp in front of the Deity while bells are rung. The priest also offers flowers, sweets and fruit. These offerings are then distributed to the devotees as a blessing from God. Hindus may visit the temple throughout the day to worship and meditate.

THE IMPACT TODAY

There are Hindu temples in nearly every country of the world

ACADEMIC VOCABULARY

indentured
under contract to work for a certain number of years

austerity
a difficult practice of self-denial and discipline

meditate
think deeply about, go within yourself or seek God within

FESTIVALS

The biggest Hindu festival of the year is **Diwali**, or Dipavali, the Festival of Lights, celebrating the victory of good over evil, light over darkness. It takes place for five days around the new moon in October/November. It also honors the return of Lord Rama to Ayodhya after 14 years in exile. Lakshmi, the Goddess of Wealth is invoked for prosperity, and Her presence is felt in every home. Hindus thoroughly clean the house, take a special bath and put on new clothes. Thousands of small lamps, including traditional clay oil lamps (pictured at right), are placed everywhere and fireworks signal hope for mankind. It is a national holiday in India and in many countries with large Hindu populations. Some Hindu festivals take place mostly at home, such as Raksha Bandhan, which is on the full moon in July/August. Sisters tie a *rakhi*, or colored thread, around the wrist of their brothers. In return, the brother gives his sister a present and promises to protect her. The *rakhi* can also be given to anyone chosen as an "adopted brother."

DINODIA

DINODIA

ANALYSIS SKILL **ANALYZING INFORMATION**

How do festivals help remind people to be more kind and generous to one another?

Hinduism's Saints, Teachers and Swamis

Hinduism has a rich history of saints and sages, both men and women. Their lives are educational and inspiring. They come from all castes. Some saints, such as Adi Shankara, have written detailed explanations of the *Vedas* and other scriptures. Other saints, such as Mirabai, Tukaram and Sambandar, taught through devotional songs. Recent saints include Sri Ramakrishna and Anandamayi Ma. Their deeply religious lives have uplifted millions of Hindus and others worldwide.

There are hundreds of thousands of religious scholars and teachers, both men and women, known as pundits. Some give spellbinding discourses on sacred scriptures, including *Ramayana* and *Mahabharata*. Tens of thousands may attend such gatherings, which include storytelling, preaching, devotional singing and drama. These events often go on for days or even a month.

Hinduism has millions of swamis and other holy persons. Swamis are unmarried men (and some women) who have taken up spiritual life full time. *Swami* means "he who knows himself." Some live in monasteries; others wander as homeless **mendicants**. Swamis are the religious ministers of Hinduism. Many swamis teach, others run large institutions that perform social service for their communities, and still others live alone and meditate long hours each day in their pursuit of divine enlightenment. Special among these are the holy gurus. *Gu* means darkness and *ru* means remover. So *guru* literally means "the one who removes darkness." These men and women are great religious teachers, some with millions of followers. Several gurus have popularized the Hindu practice of yoga by establishing training centers all over the world. No one person or institution is in charge of Hinduism. Instead, there are thousands of independent spiritual traditions, monastic orders and religious institutions.

The Yearly Festival Cycle

There are many religious festivals celebrated by Hindus each year. They are observed at home, in temples and public places. Most Hindu festivals are observed according to an ancient solar-lunar calendar. Several festivals honor the avatars of Lord Vishnu. For example, Ram Navami celebrates the birth of Lord Rama in March/April. Krishna Janmashtami, in July/August, celebrates the birth of Lord Krishna.

Mahasivaratri takes place in February/March, when devotees fast and worship the transcendent Lord Siva all night in the temple. Diwali, or Dipavali, is the biggest festival of the year. It is dedicated to Lakshmi, the Goddess of Wealth, and takes place in October/November. Navaratri is the second largest festival. It lasts nine days and takes place in September/October. It is dedicated to the worship of the Goddess, Shakti in her three forms: Durga, the Goddess of Protection; Lakshmi, the Goddess of Wealth, and Sarasvati, the Goddess of Knowledge.

Holi, in March/April, is a highly spirited festival where everyone sprinkles each other with colored water and powders. It signifies the triumph of good over evil and marks the beginning of the winter crop harvest. Vaikasi Visakham (May/June) is sacred to Hindus, Buddhists and Sikhs. Guru Purnima is a special festival to honor one's spiritual teacher, or guru. It takes place on the full moon day in July. There are also many social festivals in India, such as Pongal. It is held in January and celebrates the incoming harvest.

One special festival, the Kumbha Mela, takes place in a twelve-year cycle. Hindu saints and millions of devotees travel to certain sacred rivers at an **auspicious** time for worship. The 2001 Kumbha Mela was held at Prayag (modern Allahabad) in North India. It was attended by 70 million people, including 30 million on January 24 alone. This was the largest religious gathering ever held on the Earth.

SUMMARY

Hinduism is the oldest world religion. It accepts that there are many ways to worship God. It has endured for so long because the religion and culture have instilled in each Hindu a unique and strong sense of identity and community. The *Rig Veda* concludes, "Let there be everlasting unity and peace among all human beings."

HINDU SYMBOLS

The sacred oil lamp is used in the home and temple. Many Hindu events begin with the lighting of the lamp.

ACADEMIC VOCABULARY

auspicious
a favorable time—for the Mela, as determined by the Hindu calendar

---

Section 3 Assessment

REVIEWING IDEAS, TERMS AND PEOPLE

1. a. **List** What are the five basic practices of Hinduism?
   b. **Define** What does the bindi, red dot, signify?
   c. **Explain** How do Hindus use their home shrine room?
2. **List** What are the various kinds of priests and holy men and women in Hinduism?
3. a. **Explain** What is the year's biggest Hindu festival?
   b. **Define** What is the meaning of the rakhi bracelet?
   c. **Recall** What is special about the Kumbha Mela?
   d. **Elaborate** Why has Hinduism lasted so long?

4. **List** Make a list of three columns. In the first column write the name of a major Hindu festival. In the second, put the time of year it occurs. In the third list, what it celebrates.

FOCUS ON WRITING

5. **Understanding Hindu practices**
   Why do you think Hindus want to live near a temple?

India's Kumbha Mela, a spectacular religious festival, is the largest human gathering in history

Haridwar

Prayag

Ujjain

Nasik

Kumbha Mela Sites

HINDUISM TODAY

The Ganga River flows past the bathing steps at Haridwar in north India. In 1998, ten million pilgrims worshiped here during the months-long festival. The Kumbha Mela at Prayag in 2001 drew over 60 million Hindus.

DEV RAJ AGARWAL

AN ASSEMBLY OF HOLY MEN & WOMEN

The Kumbha Mela brings together tens of thousands of Hindu holy men (*sadhus*) and women (*sadhvis*) as well as millions of devout Hindus, all traveling long distances to experience months of worship and festivities.

MELA PRESS BUREAU

Hindu monks parade through narrow streets of Haridwar on their way to the river Ganga for a sacred, purifying bath.

MELA PRESS BUREAU

Swami Avdheshanand Giri, under the umbrella, heads a monastic order of hundreds of thousands of sadhus.

THOMAS KELLY

Two girls hold clay oil lamps on metal trays at the 2004 Kumbha Mela in Ujjain, one of Hinduism's "Seven Sacred Cities." These lamps will be used in the worship of the Kshipra River flowing behind them. Hindus often attend the Mela in large family groups composed of kids, parents, aunts, uncles, cousins and grandparents. There is something for everyone in the traditional worship and festive ceremonies.

THOMAS KELLY

During the festival, a vast tent city is set up along the river to house the sadhus. Here, devotees can meet and mingle with these holy monks, many of whom live alone in remote areas of the Himalayas.

All devotees eagerly immerse themselves three times in the sacred water. They hold on to steel chains to avoid slipping into the swift-flowing river.

A TIME TO CONSULT THE WISE

Leaders (below) gather for a summit during the 2004 Mela at Ujjain to discuss philosophy and current Hindu issues. At the 1974 Kumbha Mela, Ma Yoga Shakti (right) was named a Maha Mandaleshwar, chief religious leader, one of the first women given this high honor in modern times.

THOMAS KELLY

DEV RAJ AGARWAL

Understanding Kumbha Mela

1. **Explain:** Why do you think the Kumbha Mela attracts so many Hindus?
2. **Discuss:** In religions other than Hinduism, how do children and youth participate in festivals?
3. **Explain:** Why is bathing part of the religious ritual at the Mela? What parallels do you see in Christian baptism and Muslim washing before prayers?
4. **Discuss:** If you were at the Kumbha Mela, what questions would you ask the Hindu leaders at one of their summits?

Standards Assessment

DIRECTIONS: READ EACH QUESTION AND CIRCLE THE LETTER OF THE BEST RESPONSE

1. Evidence for what form of worship in the *Vedas* was found by archaeologists in the ruins of the Indus-Sarasvati civilization?
   A   Temple worship
   B   Worship at fire altars
   C   Devotional singing
   D   Sacred dancing

2. The Indus-Sarasvati civilization ended because:
   A   Aryans conquered it
   B   The Sarasvati River dried up
   C   There was a great famine
   D   The people died of plague

3. The Aryan Invasion theory was based upon:
   A   Biological evidence, such as DNA
   B   Archeological discoveries
   C   Language study
   D   Ancient histories

4. Which discovery was not made in ancient India?
   A   The concept of zero
   B   Surgery
   C   That the Earth orbits the Sun
   D   The moons of Jupiter

5. Evidence of Hindu temple worship can be as early as:
   A   1200 bce
   B   600 bce
   C   300 ce
   D   900 ce

6. Which of these descriptions does not apply to women in ancient India?
   A   Had fewer property rights than men
   B   Were never educated
   C   Wrote parts of the *Vedas*
   D   Paid fewer taxes

7. Which of these words does not describe the Hindu concept of the Supreme God?
   A   Creator of the universe
   B   Transcendent
   C   Immanent
   D   Jealous of other Gods

8. Hindus believe that the devas, such as Lord Ganesha or Goddess Lakshmi, are like:
   A   Archangels
   B   Nature spirits
   C   Mythical heroes
   D   Imaginary people

9. Which of the following is not used in nonviolent protests?
   A   Peaceful rallies
   B   Boycotts
   C   Strikes
   D   Vandalism

10. The Hindu scriptures include:
    A   The *Vedas, Upanishads* and *Bible*
    B   The *Vedas, Ramayana* and *Qur'an*
    C   The *Vedas, Upanishads, Ramayana* and *Mahabharata*
    D   The *Mahabharata* and the *Iliad*

11. Hindus believe that every other religion:
    A   Is an acceptable way to approach God
    B   Is wrong
    C   Is useful, but only Hindus go to heaven
    D   Is not as good because Hinduism is older

12. How many countries do Hindus live in today?
    A   20
    B   50
    C   100
    D   More than 150

13. The saints of Hinduism are:
    A   Primarily high-caste men
    B   Only people who lived a long time ago
    C   Men and women of all castes
    D   Mostly great scholars

14. The biggest religious event in the world is:
    A   The Kumbha Mela
    B   Easter Sunday in Rome
    C   The annual pilgrimage to Mecca
    D   Christmas in New York City

Hindu India: 300 to 1100 ce

VICTORIA AND ALBERT MUSEUM

This is an 8th century South Indian bronze of Supreme God Siva as Nataraja. This divine dance depicts His five cosmic powers of creation, preservation, dissolution, veiling grace and revealing grace.

What You Will Learn...

During these eight centuries, empires, religion, commerce, science, technology, literature and art flourished in India. In ways vitally important to Hindus to this day, the Hindu faith was advanced by temple building, the Bhakti Movement, holy texts and great philosophers, saints and sages.

Of Kings and Prosperity

What You Will Learn...

Main Ideas

1. Ancient Indians regarded the subcontinent as one country.
2. From 300 to 1100 ce, India was a land of prosperity whose economic, religious and cultural influence extended across Asia.
3. Empires and kingdoms dominated most of India. Toward the end of this period, more regional powers emerged.

The Big Idea

Hindu culture, Sanskrit language and imperial tradition unified India during this age.

HINDUISM TODAY'S Teaching Standards

This column in each of the three sections presents our subject outline for India and Hinduism from 300 to 1100 ce.

1. Describe the physical and linguistic geography of India, along with population figures.
2. Describe the major empires and kingdoms, including the Guptas, Vakatakas, Chalukyas, Pallavas, Rashtrakutas, Pratiharas, Palas and Cholas.
3. Discuss the importance of Sanskrit and the *Dharma Shastras* in uniting India.
4. Describe India's early Arab trade settlements and the later Islamic invasions.

If **YOU** lived then...

You live in a village in a small kingdom in central India. One day you hear that the king of a neighboring realm has attacked your king and conquered the royal city. The conquerer demands that your king pay a portion of his income. In return, he will allow your king to continue to rule, and also protect the kingdom from others.

Should your king accept the offer?

> **BUILDING BACKGROUND** The 4th-century *Vishnu Purana* describes India: "The country that lies north of the ocean and south of the snowy mountains is called Bharata, for there dwelt the descendants of Bharata. It is the land of works, in consequence of which people go to heaven, and ultimately attain oneness with God."

Understanding India

The triangle-shaped Indian subcontinent is naturally bounded by ocean on two sides and the high Himalayan mountains on the third. Hindu tradition, scriptures and the Sanskrit language link people from one end to the other of this immense and fertile area. Our period, 300 to 1100 ce, was a golden age in India. There was widespread prosperity and remarkable social stability. Advances were made in science, medicine and technology. Many Hindu saints lived during this time and magnificent temples were built. Hinduism as practiced today evolved over this glorious period of Indian history.

Geographical regions

There are three major geographical regions in India. The first region is the Indo-Gangetic Plain. This vast, fertile region stretches northeast and southwest along the base of the Himalayas. During our period, this area was heavily forested. The second region is the Deccan Plateau, bounded by the Vindhya mountain range in the north and the Nilgiri Hills in the south. It contains several major rivers and is rich in minerals. The third region is South India, the area south of the Nilgiri Hills extending to Kanyakumari at the tip of India. It has rich agricultural farm lands.

Afghanistan

Takshashila
Ghazni
Sakala
Kashmir Region
Multan
SINDHU RIVER
Sindh Region
Deval

Himalayas
Nepal
YAMUNA RIVER
GANGA RIVER
BRAHMAPUTRA RIVER
Mathura
Kannauj
Pataliputra
Kashi
Nalanda
Vikramashila

Indo-Gangetic Plain

Ujjain
VINDHYA RANGE
Bharuch
NARMADA RIVER
Valabhi
Somnath

Vanga Region
Tamralipti

Ellora
Deccan Plateau
GODAVARI RIVER
Puri

Arabian Sea

Manyakheta
Badami
KRISHNA RIVER
Amaravati

Bay of Bengal

South India
Kanchipuram
NILGIRI HILLS
KAVERI RIVER
Puhar
Thanjavur
Madurai
Kanyakumari

Sri Lanka

This satellite photo shows India's three major regions, its principal rivers and the major cities of the period 300 to 1100. India lay at the center of the bustling sea and land trade routes to Europe, Arabia, Persia, China and Southeast Asia

Language areas

India is divided linguistically into two major regions. In the north are mainly Sanskrit-based languages, such as Hindi. In the south are the Dravidian languages, such as Tamil, which include many Sanskrit words. This division cuts across the middle of the Deccan Plateau. Often today when people speak of South India, they mean the Dravidian-speaking areas. These are the modern-day states of Andhra Pradesh, Karnataka, Kerala and Tamil Nadu. During our period, regional dialects developed within both the Sanskrit and Dravidian areas. Sanskrit was the language of religion, law and government throughout India. Travelers could use Sanskrit to communicate wherever they went on the subcontinent.

Empires and regional kingdoms

In 300 ce, an estimated 42 million people lived in India, 23% of the world's population of 180 million. Approximately 60% of the Indian people lived in the Indo-Gangetic Plain. There were many towns and cities, but more than 90% of the population lived in villages.

As our period began, the Indo-Gangetic Plain again became the most important region of India, as it had been in the past. From 300 to 550, the **Imperial** Guptas established an extensive empire from the Himalayas deep into the south of India. Samudra Gupta (335-370) was the most heroic conqueror. The reign of his son, Chandra Gupta II Vikramaditya (375-414), was the most brilliant in the entire Hindu history.

Sanskrit

Dravidian

Linguistic Regions

ACADEMIC VOCABULARY

imperial
of, or relating to, an empire

The Gupta kings granted local and regional **autonomy**. The frontier states were nearly independent. The empire was responsible for security, major roads, irrigation projects and common welfare.

The Guptas created both political and cultural **pan-India** unity. India made original literary, religious, artistic and scientific contributions that benefitted the entire known world. Chinese Buddhist monk Fa-hsien (Faxian) reported in the early 5th century, "In the cities and towns of this country, the people are rich and prosperous." Hinduism thrived under the Guptas, taking forms which endure until today. Gupta culture and economy influenced much of Eurasia, notably China and Southeast Asia.

The Gupta **Empire** declined in the late 5th century because of internal strife and invasions by fierce Central Asian Hunas who ruled areas west of the Indus. The Hunas were driven back in the mid-6th century by emerging Hindu rulers.

During his 17-year journey through India, 7th century Chinese monk-scholar Hsuan-tsang (Xuanzang) wrote that there were about 70 regional powers. Many were part of the empire of King Harsha in the North

and the major empires of the South.

In the 8th century, the Rashtrakutas took control of the entire Deccan, parts of West Central India and much of the South. Between the 8th and 10th centuries, they competed with the Pratiharas and Palas for pan-India dominance. The Pratiharas at their peak ruled much of northern India. They were the first to effectively stop Arab Muslim invasions into western India, holding them in check until the 10th century. The Palas, a Buddhist dynasty centered in eastern India, reached their zenith in the early ninth century. Then the Pratiharas displaced them from much of the Gangetic Plain.

There were several large Hindu kingdoms in the Deccan and South India in our period. They included the Vakatakas, Chalukyas, Pallavas and Pandyas. Rajendra Chola I, who ruled from 1014-1044, unified the entire South. The Cholas had a large army and navy. In an effort to protect their trade routes, they subdued kingdoms as far away as Malaysia and Indonesia. Their expeditions are unique in Indian history. The Cholas dominated trade between South India and the Middle East and Europe in the West, and Southeast Asia and China

Gupta Empire: 300-550, with its capital at Pataliputra (present-day Patna)

ACADEMIC VOCABULARY

autonomy
self-rule, independence

pan-India
relating to the whole of India

empire
a group of kingdoms under one authority

plunder
property seized violence

sack
to seize all valuables and destroy building

Timeline: 300 to 1100 ce

320
Gupta dynasty flourishes through 550 during a golden age of literature, art, science and religion

Gold Coin of Chandra Gupta II

500
Bhakti Movement begins, gaining strength over the next thousand years. It was led by saints such as Sambandar of South India (at right with God Siva and Goddess Parvati)

Child Saint Samband

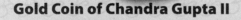

| 300 CE | 400 | 500 | 600 |

300-1000
World-famous Ajanta and Ellora Caves are created

476
Rome falls. Indian trading shifts from Europe to Arabia and the Middle East while continuing with China

542
Hindu kings defeat Hunas and end their brutal rule in central and northern India

641
Harsha, ruler of much of north India, establishes diplomatic relations with China

in the East. Indian traders brought Hindu religion and classical culture to Southeast Asia. Hindu and Buddhist kingdoms arose in present-day Malaysia, Indonesia, Thailand, Cambodia and South Vietnam.

Government and legal system

The kingdoms of India were guided by the *Shastras*, Hindu legal texts written in Sanskrit. The *Dharma Shastras*, such as *Manu* and *Yajnavalkya*, recorded laws and customs regarding family, marriage, inheritance and occupation, as well as suggested punishments for crimes. The *Artha Shastra* and *Niti Shastras* offered rules and advice on the king's behavior, war, justice, administration and business regulation. People believed that when the king was brave and just, the kingdom prospered. *Shastras*, local customs, advice of the wise and sound judgment of the king together produced sophisticated, stable and enlightened government.

Muslim invasions

Arabia, where the new religion of Islam began in 610 ce, had long traded with India. Arab merchants belonging to Islam settled peacefully in South India in the early 7th century. By 711 Arab Muslim armies had conquered North Africa, Spain and the Persian empire. They attacked India's frontiers as well. Arab Muslims conquered Sindh (now in southern Pakistan) in 712. Their further invasions were stopped by the Pratiharas, who confined Muslim rule to the Sindh region. Northwestern India remained stable under Hindu rule until the Turkish King, Mahmud of Ghazni (in modern Afghanistan), invaded India for **plunder** and the expansion of Islam. Ruling from 998-1030, Mahmud raided the country 17 times, wreaking large-scale destruction of temples, cities and palaces. The **sack** of the famed Siva temple of Somanatha in 1025 was the most horrific, involving the massacre of 50,000 defenders and the theft of fabulous wealth. This battle marked the beginning of Muslim domination of northwestern India.

Section 1 Assessment

REVIEWING IDEAS, TERMS AND PEOPLE

1. **List:** What are India's major geographic regions?
2. **Describe:** Where did most Indians live in 300ce? What was it like? Who ruled this area at that time?
3. **Explain:** How did the Cholas succeed in unifying South India and spreading Hindu culture overseas?
4. **Apply:** What do you think are some rules and advice that the *Shastras* should give for kings?
5. **Evaluate:** If you ruled a kingdom that was attacked by a more powerful empire, would you fight back or try to join the empire? Why?

FOCUS ON WRITING

7. **Analyze:** Describe the Indian empires of the time and explain why they were attacked by Mahmud of Ghazni.

712
Arab Muslims conquer the Sindh region of western India. Their further advance is halted by Hindu armies. No further conquests occur for nearly 300 years.

Thanjavur Temple

SHUTTERSTOCK

1025
Chola dynasty is at its height. Its influence extends across Southeast Asia. Builds great temples at Thanjavur and creates world-famous bronze statues of Siva Nataraja.

800	900	1000	1100

732
Charles Martel decisively stops Arab expansion into Europe at the Battle of Tours (in central France)

802
Jayavarman II founds Indianized kingdom of Kambuja in what is now Cambodia, with capital at Angkor

1025
Mahmud of Ghazni sacks Somanatha temple in western India as part of his campaigns to plunder the fabulous wealth of India and expand Islam

Somanatha Ruins

BRITISH MUSEUM

Society, Science And the Arts

If YOU lived then...

Your father is a master potter. One day a leader of the potter's guild visits from a nearby city. He says he can sell your father's wares at a better price than he gets in the village. He explains that a caravan will come periodically through the village to collect his pots. In fact, he tells your father the guild can sell all the pots the village potters can make.

Should the potters accept the guild's offer?

> **BUILDING BACKGROUND:** Scholars used to call the period from 500 to 1000 ce the Dark Ages or Medieval Period of European history. *Medieval*, a Latin word, came to mean "backward," though it really just means "middle age." Unfortunately, these terms were also applied to Indian history. In fact, Europe and—much more so—India flourished greatly in this age.

The Abundance of India

Throughout the period from 300 to 1100, India was a wealthy country. It produced a large amount of food, manufactured goods and various items for domestic and foreign trade. The nation made advances in medicine, mathematics, astronomy and metallurgy. People enjoyed prosperity, peace and freedom and achieved unprecedented artistic and culture excellence.

The richest nation in the world for over 1,000 years

Economic historians estimate that between the first and eleventh century ce, India produced roughly 30% of the world's Gross Domestic Product, or GDP. The GDP is the total value (the "gross") of everything a country or region produces. It includes the value of food, manufactured items (such as cloth, jewelry, tools and pottery) and services (such as the incomes of doctors, teachers, authors and artists). India had the highest GDP in the world for this entire period. China was the next highest, with 25% of the world's GDP. By comparison, in 1,000 ce Europe's GDP was just 11%.

Cities: centers of wealth and culture

The Indian subcontinent's population in the fifth century is estimated at 50 million, of which perhaps five million lived in cities and towns.

What You Will Learn...

Main Ideas

1. India was a wealthy country during this period.
2. Towns and villages provided economic and social structures that brought prosperity.
3. Important advances in science, technology, literature and art were made.

The Big Idea

India's towns and villages were largely self-governing.

Key Terms

Gross Domestic Product, *p. 26*
commerce, *p. 27*
varna, p. 28
jati, p. 28
panchayat, p. 29

HINDUISM TODAY'S TEACHING STANDARDS

5. Explain how India was the world's richest country during this period.
6. Describe the main features of town and village life.
7. Explain the principal advances in art, science, technology and mathematics, especially the decimal system.

The capitals where the kings lived were usually the biggest. Cities and towns grew up along important trade routes, at sea and inland river ports and adjacent to major temples and pilgrimage centers. Temples had become an important focus of life in cities and villages. They served as places of worship, scholarship, education and performing arts. City life was dynamic, diverse and fulfilling, as seen in the excerpt from an ancient poem, *The Ankle Bracelet*, on pages 10 and 11.

Larger houses were two- or three-story structures with tile roofs, built around an open-air, central courtyard. The homes of wealthy citizens had attached gardens. Cities maintained public gardens, parks and groves. Prosperous citizens were expected to be highly **sophisticated** and to lead an active social and cultural life. Ordinary citizens lived in humbler circumstances.

Then, as now, the Hindu calendar was filled with home celebrations and public festivals. Some festivals, such as Sivaratri, took place in temples. Others, like Diwali, Holi and Ramnavami, were held city-wide.

Singing, dancing and gambling were available in special city areas throughout the year. Traveling troupes of musicians, acrobats, storytellers and magicians provided entertainment.

Cities served as centers of **commerce** and were largely self-governing. A four-person ruling council included a representative from the big business community, the smaller merchants and the guilds of artisans. The fourth member, the chief clerk, was responsible for making and keeping records, such as land deeds.

The wealth of the region depended upon the abundant agricultural harvests and the diverse products of many artisans. It was in the city that this wealth was concentrated. The king and well-to-do citizens actively supported the fine arts, including literature, music, dance and drama. They promoted medicine, technology and science. They patronized the skilled jewelers, weavers, painters, metalworkers and sculptors.

ARTISTIC ACHIEVEMENT

The artisans of India produced masterpieces which included huge temples, metal and stone statues and ornate gold coins.

Three Chola-era bronze statues: Lord Vishnu (center), Bhudevi, the Earth Goddess (left), and Lakshmi, Goddess of Prosperity (right)

PHOTOS: BRITISH MUSEUM

This Gupta-era gold coin (actual size) has a horse on one side and Goddess Lakshmi on the other. It weighs about eight grams.

Sarasvati, Hindu Goddess of knowledge, music and the arts, was also worshiped in the Jain religion

SCIENTIFIC ADVANCEMENT

Among India's greatest contributions to the world are the concept of zero and counting with ten numbers. This decimal system was best explained by Brahmagupta. He was born in 598 ce and lived during the time of King Harsha. It was much easier to multiply, divide, add and subtract with the Indian system. At right you can see the English numbers and the Sanskrit they were derived from. Note how you can recognize some shapes, such as 3 and some names, such as *nava* for nine. Aryabhata (pictured here), born in 476 ce, lived in the Gupta age. He determined that the Earth is a sphere spinning on its axis. He calculated its circumference within just 67 miles. He understood and accurately predicted solar and lunar eclipses. He also made discoveries in mathematics. The Delhi Iron Pillar (lower right) is 23 feet 8 inches tall, 16 inches in diameter at the base, and weighs 6.5 tons. This victory pillar was forged in the 4th century and has stood without rusting for the past 1,700 years. Scientists have determined that an unusual chemical composition has made it rustproof. Only a few **foundries** in the world today could duplicate it.

DONALEE HOUSTON

0	shunya	೦
1	eka	१
2	dvi	२
3	tri	३
4	chatur	४
5	pancha	५
6	shash	६
7	sapta	७
8	ashta	८
9	nava	९

DINODIA

ANALYSIS SKILL | **ANALYZING INFORMATION**

Find a few English words or parts of words that are related to the Sanskrit numbers. For example, the *tri* in triangle is related to Sanskrit *tri, 3.*

ACADEMIC VOCABULARY

foundry
a workshop for casting metal

guild
an association of craftsmen who cooperate in the production and sale of goods

barter
exchange of goods or services for other goods or services (without using money)

Understanding the village

The villages, where 90 percent of the people lived, were usually surrounded by agricultural land. Each had for common use a pond or water reservoir, wells, grazing grounds and at least one temple. The year-round warm climate and monsoon rains allowed farmers to produce two crops a year. The villages enjoyed a food surplus, except when struck by natural disaster. The villages had priests, doctors and barbers and skilled craftsmen, such as carpenters, blacksmiths, potters, oil pressers and weavers. Some villages specialized in one or more trades, which were organized into **guilds**, or *shrenis*. There were daily and weekly markets in the villages and nearby towns to **barter** and sell goods.

Hindu society evolved into many *jatis*, based on specific occupations. The *jatis* are called *castes* in English. *Jatis* are grouped under the four-fold class division, or *varna*: priests, warriors, merchants and workers. A fifth group gradually developed that included scavengers, leather workers, butchers, undertakers and some tribal people. This group, about ten percent of the population, was considered "untouchable" and lived outside the city or village.

The Chinese pilgrim Fa-hsien reported that when a member of one of these castes entered a city, he had to clap two sticks together to announce his presence.

Because the *jatis* were hereditary, the families became expert farmers, craftsmen, merchants, etc. Each family in the village interacted with all other *jatis* and were bound together in a permanent relationship.

There would be a family barber, washer-man, priest, doctor, carpenter, etc., routinely serving the family needs. Thus the village was an interlocked economic unit. Each village was self-governed by an assembly of five elders, called the *panchayat*.

The central unit of the town and village was the joint family, as it is today among many Hindus. Father, mother, sons and their wives, unmarried daughters and grandchildren all lived under one roof. Land and finances were held in common, and everyone worked for the advancement of the family.

Marriages were often arranged by the parents. The boy and girl had little say in the matter, but if a couple **eloped**, the marriage was recognized. In the system called *swayamvara*, a woman, usually a princess, could choose her husband from a group of assembled suitors.

Villages were interconnected with one another, due in part to arranged marriages. The girl often came from a different village, one not more than a day's journey away. A day's journey (on foot or by bullock cart) was about 60 kilometers. Visits to relatives created an interlocking communications network through which news, technology and ideas freely flowed. Merchants, Hindu holy men and women, storytellers and pilgrims added to this network of communication and to cultural enrichment. Such **itinerants** often traveled long distances throughout India. Each village along the way offered abundant hospitality.

Science, technology and art

India's enduring prosperity allowed for great progress in science, technology and the arts. The most visible examples are the great stone temples that stand today. These temples were expertly carved using simple iron chisels and hammers.

Knowledge was taught in many schools. The world's first universities were built, including Takshashila, Nalanda, Vikrama-shila and Vallabhi. Students entered Takshashila at age 16 and studied the *Vedas* and the "eighteen arts and sciences," which included medicine, surgery, astronomy, agriculture, accounting, archery and elephant lore. One could later specialize in medicine, law or military strategy. Nalanda was described by Hsuan-tsang as a center of advanced studies with 10,000 students and 2,000 teachers.

Indian medicine, **ayurveda**, developed sophisticated systems of disease prevention, diagnosis and treatment. Widely practiced today, this holistic system aims to create and preserve health, rather than just cure disease.

From the Gupta Empire onward, India witnessed a vast outpouring of literature in the form of plays, poems, songs and epics. Performing arts were noted for portraying the nine *rasas*, or emotions: love, humor, compassion, anger, heroism, fear, disgust, tranquility and wonder.

All these achievements created what historians call a "classical age." India developed strong moral values and noble ethical principles. High standards of intellectual and artistic sophistication and refined patterns of living were set that served as models for following generations.

Section 2 Assessment

REVIEWING IDEAS, TERMS AND PEOPLE

1. a. **Define:** What is Gross Domestic Product?
   b. **Identify:** What country had the biggest GDP in the world for 1,000 years? What country was next richest?
2. a. **Explain:** Where were cities and towns located?
   b. **Analyze:** Who ran the city? Do you think this was a good system? Why?
   c. **Contrast:** Give three ways that Indian villages were different from the cities.
3. a. **Evaluate:** Do you think the system of *jatis* was a good system? How is it different from modern life?

FOCUS ON WRITING

4. **Analyze:** Why is this time a "classical age" in India?

City Life in South India

Translation by Alain Danielou

The Ankle Bracelet is an ancient **Tamil** poem. This excerpt describes the port city of **Puhar** during an annual Hindu festival. Puhar was typical of the port cities of our period.

AS YOU READ Try to visualize what the city looked and felt like.

The Sun appeared, peering over the eastern hills. He tore off the mantle of night, spread his warm and friendly rays over the pale Earth. The sunshine lighted up the open terraces, the harbor docks, the towers with their arched windows like the eyes of deer. In various quarters of the city the homes of
① wealthy Greeks were seen. Near the harbor, seamen from far-off lands appeared at home. In the streets hawkers were selling **unguents**, bath powders, cooling oils, flowers, perfume, incense. Weavers brought their fine silks and all kinds of fabrics made of wool or cotton. There were special streets for merchants of coral, sandalwood, myrrh, jewelry, faultless pearls, pure gold and precious gems.

In another quarter lived grain merchants, their stocks piled up in mounds. Washermen, bakers, vintners, fishermen and dealers in salt crowded the shops, where they bought betel nuts, perfume, sheep, oil, meat and bronzes. One could see coppersmiths, carpenters, goldsmiths, tailors, shoemakers and clever craftsmen making toys out of cork or rags, and expert musicians, who demonstrated their mastery in the seven-tone scale on the flute and the harp. Workmen displayed their skills in hundreds of small crafts. Each trade had its own street in the workers' quarter of the city.

At the center of the city were the wide royal street, the street of temple cars, the **bazaar** and the main street, where rich merchants had their mansions with high towers. There was a

GUIDED READING

Word Help

Tamil
Ancient language of South India

Puhar
A port city 240 kilometers south of modern Chennai

unguent
an ointment

bazaar
a large marketplace

① Greek merchants had homes in the city of Puhar.

Why do you think they were wealthy?

street for priests, one for doctors, one for astrologers, one for peasants. In a wide passage lived the craftsmen who pierce gems and pearls for the jewelers. Nearby were those who make trinkets out of polished sea shells. In another quarter lived the coachmen, bards, dancers, astronomers, clowns, actresses, florists, betelsellers, servants, **nadaswaram** players, drummers, jugglers and acrobats.

On the first day of spring, when the full moon is in Virgo, offerings of rice, cakes of sesame and brown sugar, meat, **paddy**, flowers and incense were brought by young girls, splendidly dressed, to the altar of the God who, at the bidding of Indra, king of heaven, had settled in the town to drive away all perils. As they went away from the altar, the dancers cried, "May the king and his vast empire never know **famine**, disease or dissension. May we be blessed with wealth—and when the season comes, with rains."

The people made merry on Indra's chosen day. Great rituals were performed in the temples of the Unborn Siva, of Murugan, the beauteous god of Youth, of Valiyon, brother of Krishna, of the dark Vishnu and of Indra himself, with His strings of pearls and His victorious **parasol**. A festive crowd invaded the precincts of the temple, where Vedic rituals, once revealed by the God Brahma, were faultlessly performed. The four orders of the Gods, the eighteen hosts of paradise and other celestial spirits were honored and worshiped. Temples of the Jains and ❷ their charitable institutions could be seen in the city. In public squares, priests were recounting stories from the scriptures of the ancient *Puranas*.

V&A MUSEUM/SHIVA DAYAL LAL OF PATNA

This 19th-century painting portrays a typical Indian food market. About 50 different items are for sale. *How many can you identify?*

GUIDED READING

Word Help

nadaswaram
a high-pitched, double-reed wooden horn

paddy
unhusked rice

famine
extreme shortage of food

parasol
here, a highly decorated, ceremonial umbrella

❷ The city had both Hindu and Jain temples.

How does this show religious tolerance on the part of the citizens?

Understanding Original Sources

1. **Comparing:** The scenes described in this poem took place over 1,800 years ago. What are the similarities and differences between the people and activities portrayed here and those of a modern city?

2. **Analyzing:** In these times, each craft or trade was the work of a separate *jati*. How many *jatis* can you identify from the crafts and trades mentioned in this poem?

Leading a Sacred Life

What You Will Learn...

Main Ideas

1. Hinduism permeated the lives of India's people.
2. A great devotional movement developed during this time.
3. The Hindu religion made it possible for anyone to reach God.

The Big Idea

India's rulers and people held a tolerant attitude toward all religions.

Key Terms

religious harmony, *p. 32*
Bhakti Movement, *p. 33*
puja, p. 33
Agama, p. 34
Purana, p. 34

HINDUISM TODAY'S TEACHING STANDARDS

8. Explain how Hindu kings maintained religious harmony.

9. Describe the Bhakti Movement and the importance of the *Puranas, Ramayana* and *Mahabharata*.

10. Describe the importance of the *Agamas* and the development of temple worship during this period.

If YOU lived then...

It is your first visit to the thriving city of Puhar. When you arrive with your parents, you see not only Hindus but also Jains and Buddhists. You observe Buddhist monks debating philosophical points with Hindus, but afterwards all having snacks together as friends. The king of Madurai, you learn, is a Hindu, but he also shows his religious tolerance by supporting Jain temples and Buddhist monasteries.

What is the value of religious harmony?

BUILDING BACKGROUND: Physical evidence of ancient culture is sparse. Wood, paper and cloth disintegrate over time; bricks and stones are recycled. This makes it hard to answer some questions about history. But scientific methods such as carbon dating and DNA analysis are giving new data and correcting wrong theories about ancient times.

Leading a Sacred Life

Daily life in villages and towns was guided by the principles of righteous living as taught in the Hindu scriptures. Every day began with a time of worship in the home shrine. Temples were the center of village and city life. Families visited them to worship God and participate in festivals and celebrations which were held throughout the year. Holy men and women were honored. One's daily work was considered sacred. The people respected all the religions.

Truth is One, paths are many

Most kings of this period were Hindus; some were Buddhists and Jains. With rare exceptions, all supported the various religions during their reign. A *Rig Veda* verse declares: *Ekam sat vipra bahudha vadanti.* "Truth is one, sages describe it variously." This means that there are different ways to speak of the One Truth that is God.

The Rashtrakuta rulers, for example, not only patronized Saivism and Vaishnavism, but also supported Jainism and Buddhism. Rulers of the period welcomed Christians, Jews, Muslims and Parsis and encouraged them to settle in their kingdoms and practice their faiths. This policy maintained religious harmony in society and even aided international trade.

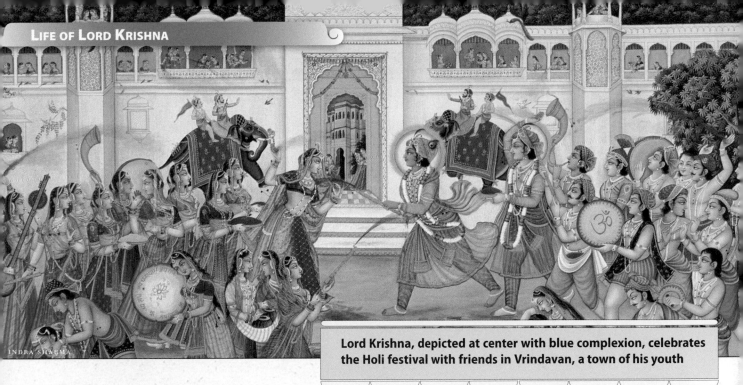

INDRA SHARMA

Lord Krishna, depicted at center with blue complexion, celebrates the Holi festival with friends in Vrindavan, a town of his youth

Evolution of temple worship

From ancient times, Vedic fire worship rites, called *yajna*, had been practiced. Families continued to perform these rites at home each day. Rulers across India held spectacular Vedic ceremonies, including coronations and other royal celebrations. Scholars believe that the devotional worship of God and the Gods in small shrines existed alongside or even predated Vedic rites everywhere, especially in South India.

Since at least the third century bce, devotional worship became increasingly popular. It eventually became the central practice of Hinduism. Some small shrines evolved into great temples with more complex worship, called *puja*. *Puja* is the ritual offering of water, food, flowers and other sacred substances to the enshrined Deity. *Yajna* rites, Sanskrit chanting and verses from the *Vedas* were all incorporated into the temple rituals.

The Bhakti Movement

Many Hindu saints of this time preached the importance of devotion to God in what is called the Bhakti Movement. **Adoration** for God, known as bhakti, stresses one's personal relationship with the Divine as a love-centered path of spiritual advancement. It complemented meditation and yoga, offering an all-embracing means to enlightenment and liberation from birth and rebirth through divine grace.

The most famous early saints of the Bhakti Movement are the **Vaishnavite** Alvars and the **Saivite** Nayanars. They came from all castes and were a voice for equality. Four of the Nayanars enjoy prominence to this day: Appar, Sundarar, Sambandar and Manikkavasagar.

While pilgrimaging from temple to temple, the Nayanars composed poems and songs in praise of the loving God Siva. These became part of a massive body of scripture called the *Tirumurai*. These passionate hymns, composed in the Tamil language, remain popular today in South India. Saints emerged all over India composing devotional songs to Siva, Vishnu, Krishna, Rama and Devi in local languages. There was a massive response to this stirring call of divine bliss.

Great teachers and philosophers, such as Ramanuja and Yamunacharya, were critical to the Bhakti Movement. They explained how to relate to God through worship.

THE IMPACT TODAY

Hindu temple worship continues to be performed in modern times, using Sanskrit chanting and following instructions from the *Agama* scriptures.

ACADEMIC VOCABULARY

adoration
deep love and respect

Saivite
worshiper of Siva

Vaishnavite
worshiper of Vishnu

ROCK-CUT TEMPLE

The Kailasanatha Temple to Lord Siva at Ellora, Maharashtra, in West India, was begun in the 8th century by Rashtrakuta King Krishna I and completed by his successor. Amazingly, it was carved out of a solid mountain of rock. It took the stone workers 100 years to remove 200,000 tons of rock. The temple, measuring 160 feet by 280 feet, was created in the South Indian style by architects of that region. It was designed to resemble Mount Kailasa, the Himalayan home of God Siva. Along the same rock cliff are 34 caves that were excavated from the solid rock between the 5th and 10th centuries. They served as monasteries and temples. Twelve were built for the Buddhists, 17 for Hindus and five for Jains. The fact that these were all built in the same complex testifies to the religious harmony and diversity of the period.

SHUTTERSTOCK

ANALYSIS SKILL **ANALYZING INFORMATION**

Why do you think the king went to so much time and expense to build this large temple?

ACADEMIC VOCABULARY

guru
teacher

avatar
the Supreme Being appearing in human form

Adi Shankara

The **guru** Adi Shankara (788-820) developed the philosophy of Advaita Vedanta during this time. In summary, his philosophy can be stated as: "Brahman (the Supreme Being) is the only truth. The world is an appearance. There is ultimately no difference between Brahman and the *atma*, or individual soul." He taught this philosophy across India. He established four monastic centers which remain influential today. His teachings and the Bhakti Movement together brought back many Jains and Buddhists to Hinduism.

Temple Worship

All over India great Hindu temples were built or expanded between 300 and 1100 ce. Many are at the center of large cities, such as Varanasi on the Ganga in the North, and Madurai in the South, and remain powerful places of worship.

In the temples, the people worshiped their chosen Deity with great devotion and paid respects to the many other enshrined Deities. The priest conducted the holy rituals, but did not stand between the devotee and God.

Temple worship was defined in great detail in the *Agamas* and parts of the *Puranas*. The refined art of building with stone, brick and other materials was the subject of the *Vastu Shastras*. These books on architecture cover temple design, town planning and house construction. All these texts are in Sanskrit. The *Agamas* include rituals and Sanskrit chants for every act connected with the temple, from its conception and construction to the details of daily worship.

Temples were central to the social and economic life of the community. Large temples also served as centers for education and training in music and dance. Over the centuries, many temples acquired agricultural land and great wealth. During festivals, thousands of people pilgrimaged to the famous temples. This flow of visitors helped the local economy and spread cultural practices and religious belief.

The *Purana* Scriptures

Puranas are dedicated to a particular Deity. Each contains a description of the origin of the universe, lists of kings, Hindu philosophy and traditional stories about the Gods and Goddesses. Among the most important *Puranas* are the *Bhagavata, Vishnu, Siva* and the *Markandeya*, especially for its *Devi Mahatmya* section. The *Bhagavata* narrates the greatness of Lord Vishnu and His ten **avatars**, of whom the two most important are Lord Rama and Lord Krishna. The *Siva Purana* extols the four-fold path leading to oneness with Lord Siva: service, worship, **yoga** and wisdom. It also explains "*Namah Sivaya*," regarded by Saivites as the most sacred of **mantras**.

The *Puranas* record an important feature of Hinduism, the **assimilation** of different ethnic and religious groups. They tell us that earlier migrants into India, such as the Greeks, Persians and central Asian peoples, including the Hunas, had been completely absorbed into Indian society and Hindu religion. Various tribes were also brought into the mainstream and their beliefs and practices assimilated. The stories of these people are recorded in the *Puranas*.

Ramayana and *Mahabharata*

You read in chapter one about the two great historical tales of India, the *Ramayana* and the *Mahabharata*. These **epics** were revised into their present form and gained popularity all over India, and beyond, during our period. They played a crucial role in the development of devotional Hinduism. Unlike the *Vedas*, which could be understood only by those who studied Sanskrit, the epics were retold into local languages. Drama, dance, song, painting and sculpture based on the epics became the main means of teaching the Hindu way of life.

During our period, Hinduism and Buddhism spread to Burma, Indonesia, Malaysia, Vietnam, Cambodia and Thailand. It was made popular in these countries through the epics and other Sanskrit texts.

Chapter Summary

The time from 300 to 1100 ce was a golden age in India. Its prosperity, stability and religious harmony encouraged scientific and artistic achievements that set standards for the entire world. Devotional Hinduism developed in a powerful manner. Through songs and stories, it brought Hindu principles and values into the languages of the common people. Temples became popular centers for worship of Gods and Goddesses. The *Puranas, Ramayana* and *Mahabharata* provided an abundant library of history, philosophy, religious practices and moral teachings in stories that were passed from generation to generation. This great devotional tradition inspired and sustained the people in their daily life, as it continues to do today.

THE IMPACT TODAY

The *Ramayana* and *Mahabharata* continue to enrich religious life. They have even been made into popular movies and TV programs.

ACADEMIC VOCABULARY

yoga
practices that bring union with God

mantra
sacred sound

assimilation
the absorption and integration of a people, idea, religion or culture into a society

epic
a long poem about herioc deeds and people

Section 3 Assessment

REVIEWING IDEAS, TERMS AND PEOPLE

1. a. **Explain:** How did Hindu rulers show tolerance?
   b. **Define:** What is bhakti?
   c. **Elaborate:** What is the purpose of the temple priest?
2. **List:** Name three important *Puranas*.
3. a. **Explain:** What does *assimilation* mean?
   b. **List:** What peoples were assimilated into Hindu society?
4. a. **Explain:** What is the Bhakti Movement?
   b. **Explain:** What caste did its saints belong to?
   c. **Elaborate:** What are the ways the *Ramayana* and *Mahabharata* are presented today?

FOCUS ON WRITING

5. **Explain:** Why do you think the Bhakti Movement became popular all across India?

Hindus celebrate more festivals each year than followers of any other religion. Let's visit a few of them.

KRISHNA JANMASHTAMI: On Lord Krishna's birthday, two teams in Mumbai compete to break pots full of red-dyed yogurt hung high above the street. They are celebrating a favorite story of Krishna's childhood. He once climbed up to steal yogurt from the pot His mother had hung high in the kitchen to keep away from the children. The scene is shown in the Suvidha banners on the lamp posts at left and right. The team in yellow is getting close to the pot and a big cash prize. Thousands of such contests are held across Mumbai during the festival.

A winning reach results in a shower of colored yogurt upon the human pyramid below.

HERE'S A REALLY COLORFUL FESTIVAL

HOLI celebrates the victory of the devout child Prince Prahlada over the demoness Holika. It falls on the last full moon of February/March. It begins with bonfires in the evening and is followed the next day by the smearing of one and all with colored powders and splashing with colored water.

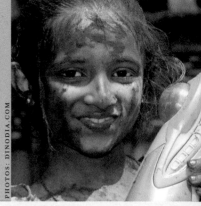

PHOTOS: DINODIA.COM

❶ "You're sure we won't get in trouble for this?" Kindergarten children pick up handfuls of powder to smear on each other.

❷ A variety of children's water guns are put to colorful use up family and friends during Holi.

DIWALI: THE FESTIVAL OF LIGHTS

DINODIA.COM

This biggest festival of the year is celebrated across India and everywhere Hindus live in the world today. It is held in October-November. Oil lamps are lit and placed in and all around the home, new clothes put on and gifts exchanged. In parts of India it also marks the beginning of the New Year. Various stories are told of its origins, all involving the victory of light over darkness, good over evil.

3 These teens are targeting each other, but any bystander, including complete strangers, could be next.

4 A temple courtyard is deluged with colored water and powders as hundreds of devotees play Holi.

THE ELEPHANT GOD'S 10-DAY-LONG CELEBRATION

Ganesha Chaturthi is held in August/September. The boy at right has purchased a clay *murti* of Ganesha which he will paint and keep on the family home altar. In Mumbai (below) huge Deities are built, paraded through the streets and on the final day immersed in the ocean.

DINODIA.COM

FOLLOW THE HINDU MOON/USHA KRIS

Exploring Religious Celebrations

1. **List:** Name major festivals from other religions and show what they have in common with Hindu festivals.
2. **Discuss:** Why do you think lamps, candles, fireworks and bonfires are a part of many festivals?
3. **Explain:** How does a festival such as Holi help keep people on good terms with each other?
4. **Evaluate:** Do you think the celebration of religious festivals benefits the community? Why or why not?

Standards Assessment

DIRECTIONS: READ EACH QUESTION AND CIRCLE THE LETTER OF THE BEST RESPONSE

1. The Indian subcontinent was united as a one country by:
   - A Hindu religion, customs and the Sanskrit language
   - B The Buddhist Pala kings of Northeast India
   - C Outside invaders who conquered the subcontinent
   - D A confederation of rulers

2. From 300 to 1100 ce, India comprised about what percent of the world population?
   - A 5%
   - B 15%
   - C 25%
   - D 35%

3. What were the Guptas not famous for?
   - A Advances in art, science and technology
   - B Creating a pan-Indian empire
   - C Suppressing the Buddhist and Jain religions
   - D A prosperous economy with strong foreign trade

4. Why did Mahmud of Ghazni invade India?
   - A To remove unjust Hindu kings from power
   - B To establish his own pan-India empire
   - C To seek revenge for an Indian invasion of his country
   - D For plunder and the expansion of Islam

5. Which is the correct list of GDPs for our period?
   - A India 50%, China 25%, Europe 5%
   - B India 20%, China 20%, Europe 20%
   - C India 11%, China 25%, Europe 30%
   - D India 30%, China 25%, Europe 11%

6. The cities of India were ruled by whom?
   - A A council representing the major interest groups
   - B A council elected by vote of all residents
   - C A hereditary ruler
   - D A military general

7. What is a *jati*?
   - A A priest, warrior, merchant or worker
   - B A group following the same hereditary occupation
   - C A group of foreign sailors
   - D A group assigned to an occupation by the king

8. Hindu villages were in close contact because:
   - A Runners daily delivered news from village to village
   - B Many women married into families of nearby villages
   - C People wrote letters to each other frequently
   - D Villages met monthly

9. Why was our time period considered a "classical age?"
   - A Greeks ruled India throughout this time
   - B Great Hindu kings conquered areas outside of India
   - C India's advances in knowledge and development of refined patterns of living
   - D The land was very prosperous

10. The city of Puhar described in the poem, *Ankle Bracelet*:
    - A Was a city intolerant of religions other than Hinduism
    - B Was an underdeveloped city
    - C Was home to many merchants and craftsmen
    - D Had little to offer by way of entertainment

11. Which of these religious groups were welcomed in India?
    - A Muslims
    - B Jews and Christians
    - C Parsis
    - D All of the above

12. Why is the Kailasa Temple in Ellora unusual?
    - A It was built from 10,000 granite blocks
    - B It was carved out of solid rock
    - C It was the largest clay brick structure in India
    - D Though made of wood, it lasted 500 years

13. The Bhakti Movement was based on:
    - A Rules set by the brahmin caste
    - B Temple worship, scriptures and devotional songs
    - C The religions of Buddhism and Jainism
    - D A royal command of the Rashtrakuta rulers

14. The *Ramayana* and *Mahabharata* influenced:
    - A Mainly the community of merchants
    - B Only the people of the Indo-Gangetic Plain region of India
    - C Mostly South India
    - D All of India and countries in Southeast Asia

CHAPTER **3**

Hinduism Endures: 1100 to 1850

The Rajput princess Mirabai devoted her life to the joyful worship of Lord Krishna. The poet saint danced and sang throughout North India.

What You Will Learn...

India responded to centuries of Muslim invasion and rule and later British colonization by both armed resistance and spiritual resolve. The country remained overwhelming Hindu despite foreign domination and religious oppression. India was one of the very few ancient societies to survive into modern times with its religion and social structure largely intact.

The Invasion Centuries

What You Will Learn...

Main Ideas

1. People today must come to terms with violent times of the past.
2. From the eighth to the eighteenth century, Muslims invaded and then ruled much of India.
3. By the nineteenth century, the British East India Company went from being traders in India to being rulers of India.

The Big Idea

India's Hindus suffered but survived centuries of Muslim and British rule.

HINDUISM TODAY'S Teaching Standards

This column in each of the three sections presents our subject outline for India and Hinduism from 1100 to 1850 ce.

1. Explain the difficulty in discussing violent historical events that continue to impact us today.
2. Describe successive invasions of India by Arabs, Turks and Mughals and the unyielding Hindu resistance.
3. Explore the founding of the Mughal Empire, its expansion and ultimate decline.
4. Explain the origins of the East India Company and how it gained control of India.

If YOU lived then...

Outside invaders have conquered the kingdom next to the one you live in. The king calls for young men to join his army. Your father decides to take the family and flee to another kingdom, away from the fighting. You may either join the army or go with the family. Your father leaves it up to you.

What do you do, and why?

BUILDING BACKGROUND: Horses thrive in Central Asia, Iran and Arabia, but they do poorly in the hot climate of the Indian plains. Invaders on horseback armed with swords and bows had an advantage over the foot soldiers and even the elephants of the Indian armies. Later, Indian kings imported horses yearly for their armies at great cost.

Understanding a Violent Past

We now enter what historians call a "difficult period" of Indian history. The difficulty is not due to any lack of knowledge. The Muslims' invasions of India were carefully chronicled by their own historians. The British also kept exacting records of their **subjugation** and exploitation of the subcontinent. We have a great deal of information, but of a disturbing nature. Muslim historians recount in detail the destruction of cities, sacking of temples, slaughter of noncombatants and enslavement of captives. British accounts reveal the mismanagement and greed that led to **famines** that killed tens of millions of people and ruined the local industry during their rule.

Nearly every country on our planet has a dark period of history it would like to forget or deny. It is difficult to study such unpleasant pasts in a way that leads to understanding, not hatred. Hindu-Muslim discord has been a fact of Indian history for over a thousand years. At the same time, there have been long periods of friendly relationship, especially at the village level. For Hindus and Muslims, coming to terms with their collective past remains a "work in progress." True **reconciliation** comes when people honestly face the past, forgive misdeeds, learn to truly respect each other's religious beliefs and traditions and promise to move forward in peace.

The Gradual Conquest of India

Muslim Arab attacks upon India began in 636 ce, soon after Islam was founded. The first successful conquest was of the Sindh region in 712, with the fall of the temple towns of Debal and Multan. By 870, Arabs conquered the Hindu kingdoms of south-western Afghanistan, then were stopped by the kings of north and northwest India.

There were three types of conquerors during this time. Some simply raided a city, robbed its wealth and left. Others defeated a kingdom, reinstated the defeated king and ordered him to pay regular **tribute**. The third and most effective conqueror annexed the captured territory to his own kingdom.

The next wave of invasions began around 1000. These attacks were not by Arabs, but by Turks from central Asia who had converted to Islam. One Turkic leader, Mahmud of Ghazni, raided India 17 times between 1001 and 1027. In each city, he looted and destroyed temples, and killed or enslaved inhabitants. Mahmud's successors periodically raided northern India, but generations of Rajput rulers denied the invaders a permanent foothold.

One of the great historians of India, A.L. Basham, wrote that warfare among Hindus was governed by "a chivalrous and humane ethical code, which discouraged such ruthless aspects of war as the sacking of cities and the slaughter of prisoners and noncombatants." The Islamic invasions introduced a brutal form of warfare which destroyed, killed and enslaved enemies at will.

In 1192, Muhammad of Ghur, also Turkic, finally succeeded in defeating Hindu rulers of the Delhi-Ajmer region and the Ganga valley. This conquest led to the establishment of the Delhi Sultanate in 1206. By 1300, the Sultanate had secured stable rule around their main strongholds of the North, and sent armies to raid as far

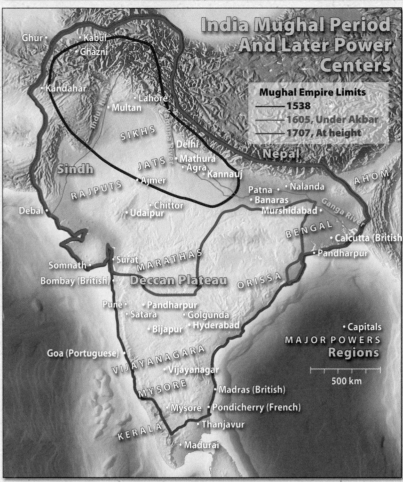

south as Thanjavur and Madurai. But these regions were not annexed. Hindu rule generally continued in Rajasthan, Gujarat and thrived in the entire South, notably within the Vijayanagar Empire (1336-1665). Areas with natural protective boundaries, such as Kashmir, Nepal, Assam, Orissa and Kerala, were less subject to raids.

By 1220, the Mongol emperor Genghis Khan had created the largest empire the world had ever seen, conquering Asia from China to Iran. In 1398, a Muslim descendant, Timur, attacked Delhi because he felt its Muslim ruler was too tolerant of

ACADEMIC VOCABULARY

subjugation
to bring under control by force

reconciliation
to restore friendly relations

famine
extreme shortage of food

tribute
payment made by one ruler to another

Hindus. In just one instance alone, he killed 100,000 Hindu captives. In 1504, Babur, a descendent of both Genghis Khan and Timur, seized Kabul. This gave him a base to attack India. He overwhelmed both the sultan of Delhi (in 1526) and the Rajput confederacy (in 1527) to found the Mughal Empire. His army was the first in India to use **matchlocks** and field cannons.

Babur's grandson, Akbar, became emperor in 1556. He expanded the Mughal Empire over northern India and part of the Deccan by entering into alliances with Hindu kings, particularly the fierce Rajputs. Akbar's rule was noted for its religious harmony. Unfortunately, his successors did not inherit his tolerance. Akbar's great-grandson, Aurangzeb, destroyed temples and reimposed the *jizya* religious tax on Hindus.

By the mid-eighteenth century, the Mughal Empire had declined. The Sikhs, Jats, Rajputs, Marathas and the Empire's own provincial governors (called nawabs) had asserted their independence, leaving no strong central government in India. The regional Muslim rulers continued to oppress Hindus, but less harshly than the centralized Muslim governments of Delhi had.

The Colonial Period

In 1600 a group of English merchants set up the East India Company to buy and sell goods between Britain, India and other eastern countries. They arrived in India as businessmen, not conquerors, and built major trading posts at Surat, Bombay, Madras and Calcutta. Over time, they **fortified** their posts and developed private armies for defense, paid for with the immense profits of their trade. They hired Hindus and Muslims as soldiers, called *sepoys,* who served under British officers.

Emboldened by their strength, the British proceeded to **meddle** in local politics. They gained power and profit by playing one rival against another. The French, especially in South India, did the same. If one king was supported by the French, the Company would back his rival as a way of weakening the French position. But they wanted still more. Robert Clive, commander of the Company's army, conspired to overthrow the Nawab of Bengal, which led to the Nawab's defeat in the Battle of Plassey in 1757.

Mir Jafar, the new Muslim ruler of Bengal rewarded Clive's support with huge gifts and a promise to favor the Company. But things

ACADEMIC VOCABULARY

matchlock
an early type of rifle

fortify
to build walls, towers and gate to protect from attack

meddle
to interfere in someone else's affairs

alliance
an agreement to work together

puppet ruler
a state ruler who is actually controlled by another ruler

Timeline: 1100 to 1850 ce

1193
Buddhist university at Nalanda is destroyed by Bakhtiyar Khalji, a Turk; soon afterwards Buddhism severely declines in India

1230–60
Surya Temple is built in Konark, Orissa, for the Sun God, Surya

Sun Temple Orissa

1350
Appaya Dikshitar, South Indian philosopher-saint, compiles a priest manual still used today

1398
Kabir is born; preaches unity of all religions

Guru Nanak

146
Guru Nanak, founde of Sikhism, is bor

| 1100 CE | 1200 | 1300 | 1400 | 1 |

1030
Arab scholar Al-Biruni writes extensive account of Indian religion, science and geography

1221
Invading Mongols under Genghis Khan reach India's border; Mongol raids continue into 14th century

1270
Maratha Vaishnava saint Jnaneshvara and Namdeva are born

Jnaneshvara

1398
Turkic warrior Timur conquers Delhi, killing tens of thousands of residents and carrying off great wealth and many slaves

did not go well, and following the battle of Buxar in 1764 the Company gained control of Bengal's revenues. A few years later they became the direct rulers and ruined the region with heavy taxes, unfair trade restrictions and corrupt practices.

The Company seldom launched a direct attack to conquer a region of India. Rather, they entered into treaties, **alliances** and other deals with local rulers, exploiting the divisions among them. Along the way, they defeated several heroic kings, such as the Muslim king Tipu Sultan of Mysore, and eventually conquered the powerful Marathas and Sikhs after many battles. In this manner, by 1857, they achieved direct rule over much of India and controlled the rest through **puppet rulers.**

Why Did the Muslims and the British Win?

Most historians agree that the Hindu kings simply failed to realize the danger they faced and thus did not mount a common defense. Historians also blame the caste system, saying that people relied solely on the warrior caste to do the fighting. Basham shows this explanation to be inaccurate, as all castes were present in Indian armies. Also, he points out, Muslim kingdoms themselves were overrun by subsequent invaders, such as Timur and Nadir Shah, putting up no better defense than the earlier Hindu kings.

Basham explains that each new invader succeeded by virtue of superior military organization, strategy, training, weapons, horses and mobility. With these they overpowered the large but cumbersome Indian armies, Hindu and Muslim alike, which failed to adapt to new methods of warfare. The British also possessed great military skill and modern weapons, a result of their wars in Europe at the time. The Indian rulers failed to recognize and counter the brilliant British strategy and tactic of conquering a region by exploiting internal divisions among its rulers and only occasionally using its own armed forces in an outright invasion.

Section 1 Assessment

REVIEWING IDEAS, TERMS AND PEOPLE

1. **Explain:** How do we know so much about the destruction in India under the Muslims and British?
2. **Describe:** What are three different ways that invading forces could profit from their conquests?
3. **Contrast:** How was the Muslim style of warfare different from that of the Hindus?
4. **Synthesize:** How could Indian kings have better fought the Muslim invaders and the British empire builders?

FOCUS ON WRITING

5. **Analyze:** How can studying the history of violence in India be useful in helping to bring about a more peaceful world today?

sidasa

1574
Tulsidasa writes popular Hindi version of *Ramayana*

1688
Mughal Emperor Aurangzeb demolishes all temples in Mathura, said to number 1,000, and many in Varanasi

Tyagaraja

1780–1830
Golden era of Carnatic music under Tyagaraja, Muthuswami Dikshitar and Syama Sastri

1834
The first indentured Indians are sent to British plantations abroad: Mauritius, Guyana and the West Indies

1835
Lord Macaulay makes English the official language of schools in India; the teaching of Sanskrit was drastically curtailed

1600

1700

1800

1857

1541
Jesuit missionary St. Francis Xavier arrives in Goa; eventually calls for an Inquisition which leads to many deaths and forced conversions

1674
Shivaji founds Maratha Empire; frees large areas from Muslim control

1699
Guru Gobind Singh founds Sikh Khalsa order, militarizing his followers

1764
British East India Company takes direct rule of Bengal; a devasating famine occurs in 1770

1857
Hundreds of thousands of Indian soldiers revolt in widespread uprising called India's First War of Independence or the Sepoy Mutiny. After brutal suppression, the British Crown takes formal control of India

Surviving a Time of Trial

What You Will Learn...

Main Ideas

1. Most Muslim rulers were intolerant of other religions, with a few exceptions, such as Akbar.
2. Muslims and Catholics alike worked to convert India's Hindus.
3. During this difficult era, Hinduism remained strong due to the influence of culture and saints.

The Big Idea

Most Hindus remained passionately devoted to Hinduism despite centuries of persecution

Key Terms

polytheism, p. 48
Sufism, p. 49
Ajlafs, p. 49

 HINDUISM TODAY'S TEACHING STANDARDS

5. Describe how the saints of the Bhakti Movement were able to inspire Hindus to new levels of religious devotion.

6. Give examples of how religious loyalty and devotion inspired Hindus to resist conversion and alien rule.

7. Analyze the rationale and strategies behind attempts to forcibly convert Hindus to Islam and Christianity.

If YOU lived then...

An army of the Muslim emperor Aurangzeb has just destroyed the temple in your Hindu village. The emperor has also reimposed a heavy tax on Hindus. Your father must always carry a receipt showing he paid the tax or else he could be punished. If your family converts to Islam, he won't be forced to pay the tax.

Do you think your family should convert?

BUILDING BACKGROUND: The Roman Catholic Inquisition took place in the Portuguese trading colony of Goa from 1560 to 1812. Church officials arrested, tortured, tried and executed Hindus, Jews, Muslims and Catholics for breaking Church laws, including restrictions against practicing any religion other than Roman Catholicism.

Hinduism Under Non-Hindu Rule

In about 1030, the Muslim scholar Al-Biruni wrote, "The Hindus believe with regard to God that He is eternal, without beginning and end, acting by free will, almighty, all-wise, giving life, ruling, preserving." He explained, "According to Hindu philosophers, liberation is common to all castes and to the whole human race, if their intention of obtaining it is perfect." He described Hindu beliefs, scripture and practices that were little different than those of today. He observed that Hindus were not inclined to war with others for religious reasons and praised India's religious tolerance.

Al-Biruni noted, with approval, that the Muslim raids had "utterly ruined the prosperity of the country." Historians today estimate that between 1000 and 1100 ce, 20 million Indians—ten percent of the population—perished. By the 16th century, tens of millions more died through war and famine, while tens of thousands of temples had been destroyed. Hindus survived this long period of adversity through devotion to God and continued loyalty to community and tradition.

Responding with Devotion

The Bhakti Movement, explained in Chapter Two, was a powerful force throughout our period all over India. It stressed one's personal relationship with God and offered many spiritual practices individu-

In a joyous festival, the Deity is paraded in a giant chariot, pulled by men holding two thick ropes. Hindus delight in sacred festivities, which bless the community and strengthen their shared faith.

als could perform on their own. By sitting alone under a tree and chanting the name of Rama, singing bhajana or meditating on God, the common Hindu could find the spiritual strength to endure hardship and **persecution**.

The great philosophers Madhva (1017-1137) and Ramanuja (1238-1317) were forerunners of popular saints during our period who strengthened Hindus and discouraged conversion. An early Vaishnava saint, Jayadeva (c. 1200), wrote the famous *Gita Govinda*, popular in Orissa and Bengal. Among the Vaishnava saints from Maharashtra were Jnaneshvara (1275-1296), Namdeva (1270-1350), Eknatha (1548-1600), Tukarama (1598-1649) and Samartha Ramdasa (1606-1682).

In North India, Swami Ramananda (ca 1400-1470) promoted the worship of Lord Rama, praising him as "Hari," a name of Vishnu. Ramananda discouraged caste, saying, "Let no one ask about another's caste or with whom he eats; he who worships Hari is Hari's own."

Two traditions arose from Ramananda's popular teachings. One group, including Nimbarka (13th century), Chaitanya (1486-1534), Surdasa (1483-1563), Mirabai (1503-1573) and Tulsidasa (1532-1623), emphasized worship of the personal God. They were enlightened persons filled with a sense of divine **ecstasy**. Vaishnavas especially revere Chaitanya and Mirabai as divine beings.

A second tradition began with Ramananda's disciple Kabir (1398-1518). He was adopted as a child and raised by a low-caste Muslim, a weaver. He wrote hundreds of spiritual poems in Hindi, the language of the people (rather than Sanskrit). His poems are easy to understand, even today, and millions still follow his teachings. Kabir's philosophy, mostly drawn from Hinduism, was simple and direct. It appealed both to Hindus and Muslims. He rejected the caste system and ridiculed many Hindu and Muslim religious practices. Seeking to promote religious harmony, Kabir taught that there is only one God for all religions.

The Sikh religion was also a powerful force. Its founder, Guru Nanak (1469-1539), taught, "Realization of Truth is higher than all else. Higher still is truthful living." He emphasized the continuous recitation of God's name and declared that meditation is the means to see God, who

Shivaji honors his guru by touching his feet

A. MANIVEL

SAINT AND KING

At the time of Shivaji's birth in 1627, the Marathas had been under Muslim domination for hundreds of years. At age 17 this courageous Maratha warrior led his first military campaign, capturing the Torna Fort from the Bijapur Sultanate in 1645. Within ten years, he gained control of enough territory to alarm Mu-

ghal Emperor Aurangzeb, who sent a series of large armies to attack him. But Shivaji's smaller, fast-moving and well-armed forces proved difficult to overcome. Unlike earlier Hindu kings, Shivaji made use of modern means of warfare and even developed a navy. In 1674, he founded the Maratha Empire. Seventy years after his death in 1680, the Maratha armies pushed Mughal forces out of much of central India, leaving the Mughal Empire permanently weakened.

Shivaji's guru, Samartha Ramdasa, gave him spiritual advice and helped inspire the Maratha people toward freedom. Ramdasa had 1,100 disciples, each an excellent preacher, including 300 women. Ramdasa taught devotion to Lord Rama, especially through chanting the mantra *"Shree Ram, Jaya Ram, Jaya Jaya Ram"*—"Victory to Lord Rama." By one account, Shivaji offered Ramdasa his entire kingdom, which Ramdasa returned to him to rule in the name of Lord Rama.

German scholar Max Weber wrote in the 19th century, "Shivaji was no bigot and allowed equal freedom to all faiths. He was served as zealously by the Muslims as by the Hindus. He built a mosque opposite his palace for the use of his Muslim subjects." While Shivaji was not above sacking an enemy's city if he needed the money, he did not kill noncombatants, take slaves or damage Muslim holy sites.

is **omnipresent**. Like Kabir and Ramananda, Guru Nanak discouraged ritual worship and caste discrimination.

Nine Sikh gurus followed Nanak. The eighth, Tegh Bahadur (1621-1675), was executed by Aurangzeb for defending religious freedom. His son and successor, Gobind Singh, transformed the Sikhs into a warrior community called the Khalsa. Gobind Singh decreed that he was the last Sikh guru and after his death the *Guru Granth Sahib*, their holy scripture, would be the guide. From that time forward, the Sikhs have been an influential political and military force in North India.

As you have studied, South India largely escaped the oppressive Muslim domination of North and Central India. To this day the South retains the most ancient Hindu culture and has many grand temples. Influential saints of the time include Meykandar, Arunagirinathar, Tayumanavar, Vallabhacharya and Kumaraguruparar.

Other religious movements also

flourished during this period such as Kashmir Saivism, Natha saints and the Gorakha Panthi yogis. They all were part of India's ongoing vibrant religious spirit.

The Conqueror's Religious Goals

The Arab and Turkic Muslim invaders who swept across the Middle East, Africa, Central and South Asia were intent on religious domination, demanding conversion from those they conquered. They made an exception for "People of the Book," Christians and Jews, because certain parts of the *Torah* and the *Bible* are regarded as revealed scripture by the Muslims as well. They did not force Christians and Jews to convert, but humiliated them and imposed the *jizya* tax.

The Muslims treated Hindus as *kafirs*, lowly non-believers. The Christians judged Hindus to be **polytheists**, and some, as in Goa, used violence to convert them. Muslims and Christians both consider monotheism (the belief that there is only one God) to be the right conviction. As explained in

Chapter One, Hindus see no contradiction in believing in One Supreme God while also worshiping the Gods and Goddesses. But this is unacceptable to Muslims and Christians, and resulted in dreadful persecution and killing during this period.

Centuries of Conversion Attempts

Before the Arabs, all foreign invaders, including the Greeks and Huns, were eventually absorbed into mainstream Hindu society. This was also true of many tribal communities within India. The Muslim rulers—with the exceptions of Akbar and some others—made great effort to convert their Hindu subjects. They used persuasion, heavy taxes, legal discrimination and force, but had only limited success.

Christian conversion efforts in India, though sustained and sometimes vigorous, were not very successful. The East India Company found missionary efforts bad for business and did not encourage them.

At their worst, invaders and later rulers destroyed Hindu temples and killed those who would not convert. According to the Muslim accounts of the time, thousands of temples were looted and torn down, including hundreds at major **pilgrimage** destinations, such as Somnath, Mathura, Vrindavan and Varanasi. Many mosques were built on the same sites from the temple materials.

Among the Muslims, the Sufi preachers were most responsible for making converts. Sufism is a **mystical** tradition within Islam, with some elements similar to the Bhakti Movement. Sufism was much stronger during this period than it is today. Sufis worked closely with Muslims rulers and helped secure their rule by converting conquered people to Islam. Many persons captured and enslaved during raids on Hindu towns and villages converted to Islam knowing they would be treated better or even released.

The caste system was a main obstacle to conversion. It guaranteed to Hindus a secure identity and place in their community, which they would lose by converting. Also, other religions did not appeal to them either philosophically or culturally. Some low-caste Hindus were tempted to convert to improve their social status. But, in fact, converts to both Christianity and Islam retained their caste position.

Even today, Indian Muslims who claim foreign ancestry—the descendants of Arabs, Turks, Afghans, etc.—are called Ashrafs and have a higher status than Hindu converts, who are called Ajlafs. The Ajlafs are divided into occupational castes, just as are Hindus. Likewise, Christian converts retained their caste status. The lowest—the Untouchables, or Dalits—even have separate churches and graveyards.

The Common Man's Plight

Altogether, the common Hindu did not fare well during this time. He faced military attacks, discrimination as a *kafir*, oppressive taxes and sustained pressure to convert. Hindu rulers collected from farmers a tax of one-sixth of their crop. Under Muslim and British rule, taxes soared to as much as one-half, plunging the people of the once wealthy country of India into poverty.

ACADEMIC VOCABULARY

mystical concerned with the soul or spirit, rather than material things

pilgrimage to travel to a special religious place

Section 2 Assessment

REVIEWING IDEAS, TERMS AND PEOPLE

1. **Explain:** What evidence do we have that Hinduism in 1030 was similar to today's Hinduism?
2. **Analyze:** What are some reasons for Kabir's continued popularity in India?
3. **Explain:** How did Shivaji's faith and religious tolerance help him lead the Maratha people against the Mughals?
4. **Analyze:** Why do Hindus see no contradiction between worshiping the Supreme God and revering many Gods?

FOCUS ON WRITING

5. Even when threatened, many Hindus refused to convert to another religion. Why did they choose to resist?

Hindu Games

Snakes and Ladders

A. MANIVEL

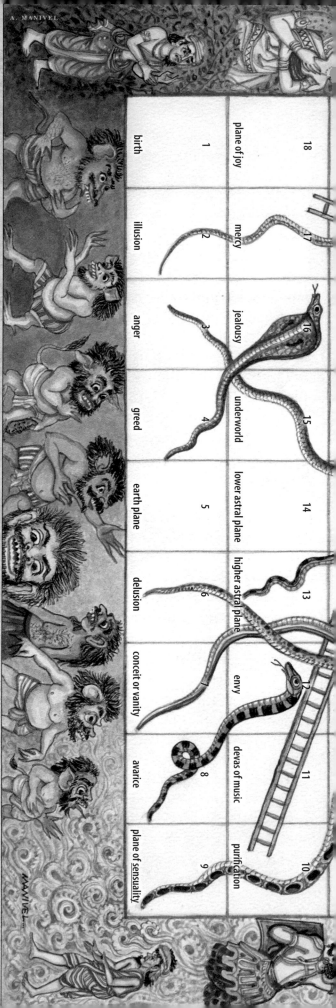

The Western children's game Snakes and Ladders, or Chutes and Ladders, comes from the Indian game for adults called Gyan Chaupar, the "Game of Knowledge." Gyan Chaupar teaches the Hindu spiritual path to moksha, which is liberation from reincarnation. There are 72 numbered squares on the board listing various virtues, vices, states of consciousness and planes of existence. The ladders start from squares with virtues, such as devotion, and move the player up the board. Snakes are found on squares of vices, such as jealousy, and take the player back down the board.

Play begins at square one in the lower left corner. In the old days, the player threw six cowrie shells on the floor. The number of shells that landed upright indicated the number of squares to

move forward. Nowadays dice are used. If the player lands on a ladder, he jumps to the square at the top of the ladder. If he lands on the head of a snake, he slides back down the snake to a low square. The object of the game is to land exactly on square 68, the center of the top row. This square represents liberation from rebirth and entry into heaven. If he lands past 68, he continues to play until he reaches 72, which takes him back to 51 for another try. The game is an entertaining way to learn about making progress on the spiritual path. By cultivating a virtue, such as devotion, one advances. By falling prey to egotism, one goes backwards.

Play the game online or download the board and full instructions at www.hinduismtoday.com/resources/snakesandladders.

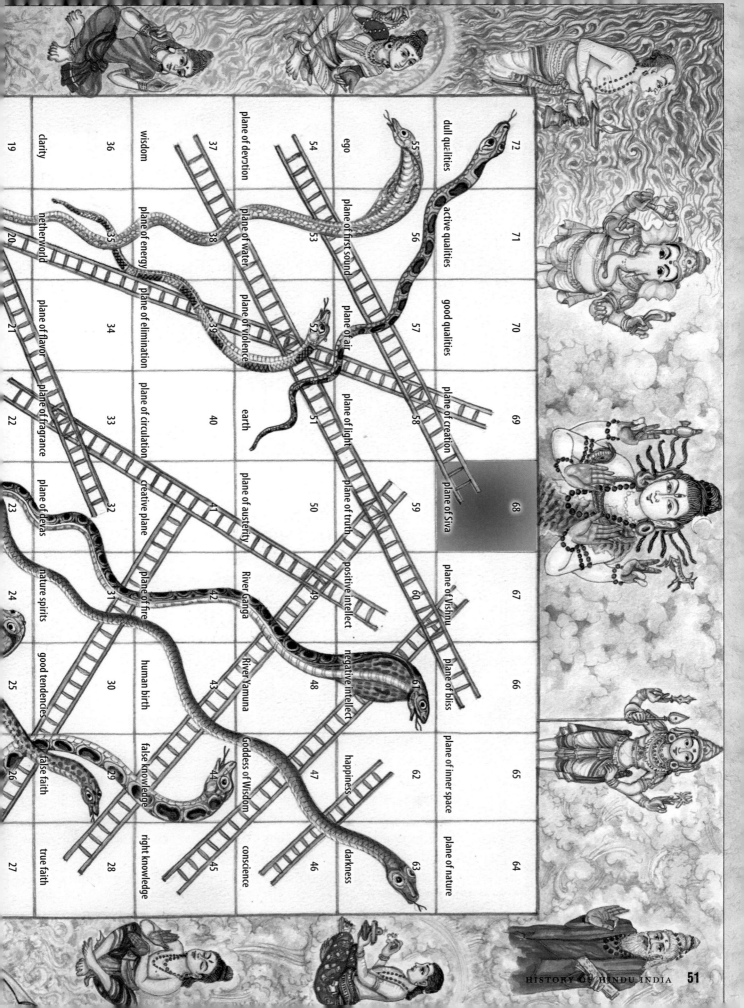

Music, Art, Dance and Architecture

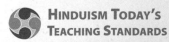
If YOU lived then...

Your father is an artist hired by Mughal Emperor Akbar in Delhi. The emperor has brought great painters from Persia. He wants to develop a new art style. You have been an apprentice to your father for several years now, but now you both must learn a new artistic style. Your father thinks it will be valuable to learn from the Persians.

How do you feel about learning the new art form?

BUILDING BACKGROUND: The arts, such as painting, music, dance and architecture, are essential parts of every culture. Flourishing civilizations develop new artistic styles over time. Fresh ideas appear and blend with old traditions, allowing artists to express the culture, thoughts and emotions of the time in beautiful, uplifting works.

Artistic Achievements

Art within Hindu India was already highly developed prior to the Arab, Turkic and Mughal invasions. Some art forms, such as music and dance, were less affected by these invasions, especially in the South where Hindu rule was the norm. In the North, Persian building design, with its arches and domes, became common, and in painting, the Mughal emperors stimulated a harmonious blending of composition and method, thus creating the Indo-Islamic art style.

A Rich History of Music

India has always had an extraordinarily diverse musical scene. This ranges from the complex works of the classical tradition to the villagers' simple work songs and devotional hymns in local languages. Temple stone workers, for example, sing together to coordinate the effort of moving a heavy stone. At a certain point in the song, all apply perfectly timed force to their iron pry bars. In this way, stones weighing tons can be moved by hand. To this day, Hindu men and women sing devotional songs to accompany and ease their daily tasks.

There is within Hinduism a long tradition of *bhajana* and *kirtana,* call-and-response devotional singing of simple songs, usually in small groups with musical accompaniment. *Katha* is a popular form of storytelling, occurring in multiple sessions, often spanning many days. A highly skilled storyteller will recount episodes from sacred texts, such as the *Ramayana*, then lead the audience in singing related *bhajanas*.

Alongside these basic musical traditions is India's classical Carnatic music. Three great innovators of this ancient system lived in South India in the late 18th and early 19th centuries: Tyagaraja, Muthuswami Dikshitar and Syama Sastri. They **systematized** and improved upon the existing framework of raga and tala, the essentials of Indian music. Hindustani is a related musical system that arose in the North as musicians blended Persian elements into the Indian tradition.

First, the composer selects a raga in which to write his song. A raga is a pattern of notes upon which a melody is made. Ragas include notes from the seven-note Indian scale (*sa, ri, ga, ma, pa, dha, ni*) as well as microtones, which are like the sharps and flats of Western music, only more numerous. This multiplicity of tones allows for the creation of thousands of ragas. Next, the composer selects a tala, or rhythmic pattern. Talas

range from the simple and most common eight-beat Adi tala to elaborate rhythms such as the Dhamar tala, composed of 14 beats divided as 5, 2, 3 and 4.

Songs were written in Sanskrit and increasingly in the regional languages, such as Hindi, Telegu and Tamil. Singers and musicians **improvise** upon the basic melody while keeping within the chosen raga and tala. The results are always creative, akin to the improvisations in Western jazz. This is one key way that Indian classical music differs from Western classical music, which is usually played exactly as it was composed.

A Meeting of Art Styles

The Mughal emperors were responsible for a major advancement in painting which eventually influenced much of India. Earlier Muslim rulers started the process by bringing artists to India to illustrate the elaborate handwritten books of the time (see top left on page 14). These painters had been influenced earlier by Chinese artists who were brought to Persia by conquering Mongols.

THE IMPACT TODAY

Modern katha performers attract crowds of thousands in the US and England, and hundreds of thousands in India.

ACADEMIC VOCABULARY

systematize
to arrange in an orderly fashion

improvise
in music, to create and perform spontaneously

INDIA'S MUSICAL INSTRUMENTS

Cymbals, drums, horns and stringed instruments commonly accompany the singer in the various types of Indian music. In concerts, the singer and the drum or horn player will engage in a kind of duet, with each improvising upon the other's melody line and rhythm.

The double-sided drum, *mridangam*, is popular in South India

Tyagaraja, Muthuswami Dikshitar and Syama Sastri. At left is the Sarasvati Vina, with 24 frets, four playing strings and three drone strings. The other two instruments are the four-stringed tambura. In the background are the Divinities of music.

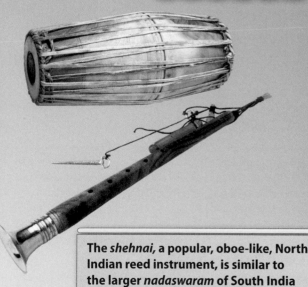

The *shehnai*, a popular, oboe-like, North Indian reed instrument, is similar to the larger *nadaswaram* of South India

V&A MUSEUM

V&A MUSEUM

EHRENFELD COLLECTION

Top left: a page from a 1330 ce Persian manuscript in the style Akbar encouraged. Top right: a watercolor painting of a scene from the Ramayana from Bengal is typical of the two-dimensional, flat style of most earlier Indian art. Above: this portrait of Rajput Raja Aniruddha Singha, painted in Rajasthan in the early 1700s, is typical of the Mughal school which evolved from the blending of earlier styles.

The Mughal Emperor Akbar, trained in art as a child, encouraged a true synthesis of forms. He commissioned craftsmen by the hundreds in an almost factory-like setting under his Royal Bureau of Books. This enterprise, headed by the great Persian artists, Khwaja Abdus Samad and Mir Sayyid Ali, resulted in major artistic innovations.

As the Mughal Empire declined, this huge community of artists lost their rich patronage. The last emperor, Aurangzeb, dismissed the artists and banned music and dance. He judged their work contrary to Islamic teachings that prohibit the depiction of religious themes in any art form. Hindu and Muslim artists turned to independent local rulers across India for support. Many applied the new techniques to Hindu subjects, especially illustrating the *Mahabharata* and stories of Lord Krishna.

Indian painting before this time was two-dimensional, as seen in the example at top left. The new style adopted typical Indian colors, used delicate brush lines (some made with a brush of a single squirrel hair) and introduced better lighting effects. Advancements were also made in the preparation of pigments and paints, allowing for a greater range and depth of color.

During the British rule, a blending of painting styles was attempted between Indo-Islamic and European art. The result, called Company style, tended toward realism, and was later displaced by the invention of photography.

Architecture

In South India during this period, the art of temple building reached its peak. In fact, Hindu temples today are still built according to the styles developed at this time, following principles from the ancient *Agama* texts. In North India, Hindu architecture was eventually strongly influenced by Persian design, especially the use of the dome and arch. The most spectacular construction during the period was the Taj Mahal, among the world's most elegant buildings. Built in white marble by Shah Jahan to entomb his beloved wife, the Taj, with its immense domes and towering minarets, is Persian

India's Sacred Dance

Religion Through Movement

Bharatanatyam and the related dances Kuchipudi and Odissi come from the ancient temple dances of South India, described in the 2,000-year-old *Natya Shastra*. Originally, dance, accompanied by classical Indian music, was one of the sixteen offerings made during the ritual worship called puja. Indian dance is not simply entertainment, but a religious experience both for the dancer and the audience. Early dance tradition used improvisation, as does Indian music, but today the choreography is usually set. Most dances are depictions of religious stories, told through poses, movements and dozens of meaningful hand gestures called mudras.

When the first Bharatanatyam dancers came to Europe in 1838, a reviewer wrote, "The dancers of all Europe dance with their feet, but that is all. The Indians dance in a different manner. They dance with their whole frame. Their heads dance, their arms dance. Their eyes, above all, obey the movement and fury of the dance. Their feet click against the floor; the arms and the hands flash in the air; the eyes sparkle; their mouths mutter; the whole body quivers."

COURTESY KANISHKA PATEL

DMITRY RUKHLENKO

A Bharatanayam dancer in the pose of Siva Nataraja; (left) hand gestures, called mudras: picking flowers, greeting, lotus

in design with many Hindu elements. Completed in 1653, it took 20,000 craftsmen working 22 years to build and was a great drain on the treasury. Shah Jahan was overthrown and imprisoned by his son, Aurangzeb, shortly after its completion.

not break down under the alien rule, so the social structure remained stable. Most Hindus did not convert to Islam, despite heavy pressure. The arrival of the East India Company changed the political situation. By force and skillful tactics, the British slowly gained complete control of India.

ACADEMIC VOCABULARY

Nataraja
"King of Dance," a form of Lord Siva

Chapter Summary

Beginning in 1100, Muslim armies conquered vast regions of India. Despite repeated defeats, the Rajput and other Hindu rulers refused to surrender. South India, far from the Muslim capitals of Delhi and Agra, escaped the unceasing warfare and foreign dominance that beset North India, suffering only periodic raids. Wherever Hindus were conquered, resistance continued, mainly on a social and religious level. The caste system did

Section 3 Assessment

Reviewing Ideas, Terms and People

1. **Describe:** What are the roles of raga, tala and improvisation in Indian classical music?
2. **Analyze:** What were some of the advancements made in painting under the Mughals? What made these advancements possible?
3. **Contrast:** How did the architecture of this period differ in North and South India and why?

Focus on Writing ✎

4. **Synthesize:** How does the mixing of cultures result in new artistic styles? Give examples from your society.

India's dance traditions are living expressions of ancient religious stories

DINODIA.COM

This is Pung Cholom, a dance from Manipur, in India's northeastern corner. These boys first learned to play the double-headed pung drum, then how to dance while playing it—a complex feat indeed! This is one of India's most energetic dances.

Most Indian dances include the nine basic emotions: love, joy, wonder, peace, anger, courage, compassion, fear and disgust. At right a Bharata Natyam dancer demonstrates five of them.

fear

wonder

KATHAKALI: This dance form from Kerala is famous for its elaborate costumes and makeup, which take hours to apply. The lamp in front is always present (in the old days it helped illuminate the dance). The stools are props used during the performance. The singer in the back is narrating the story. The dance dramas are often taken from the epic *Mahabharata*. Performances used to run all night, but are now about three hours long.

compassion   peace   disgust

CLASSICAL AND FOLK DANCES

In 1991, the Indian Post Office released stamps commemorating four of the country's folk dances: (clockwise from top left) Valar, Kayang, Velakali and Hozagiri. (right) A 2009 Kathak performance by Chetna Noopur at Noopur Performing Art Centre, Bengaluru.

Dance Tradition

1. **Interpret:** Why do you imagine India developed such a rich array of dance forms?

2. **Discuss:** What advantages would watching a religious dance drama have over reading the drama in a book?

3. **Explain:** How do a dancer's facial expressions and hand gestures help tell a story?

4. **Analyze and debate:** What role does dance play in conveying Hinduism from one generation to the next?

CHAPTER 3

Standards Assessment

DIRECTIONS: READ EACH QUESTION AND CIRCLE THE LETTER OF THE BEST RESPONSE

1. We need to understand even unpleasant history because:
   A   We can then punish the people responsible
   B   It helps us learn to live in peace today
   C   It helps us see that some religions are bad
   D   We should never forgive our attackers

2. What military advantage did Muslim invaders have?
   A   Support from people in the invaded regions
   B   Many more soldiers than the Indian kings
   C   Bigger elephants and more of them
   D   Horses, better weapons, tactics and training

3. Why is the rule of Mughal Emperor Akbar remembered as exceptional?
   A   He destroyed many Hindu temples
   B   He created the largest empire in the world
   C   He was tolerant of other religions
   D   He formed strong alliances with British merchants

4. How did the British East India Company gain control of India?
   A   They set up puppet rulers under their control
   B   They created their own army
   C   They played one ruler against another
   D   All of the above

5. How did the Bhakti Movement help preserve Hinduism?
   A   It strongly supported the caste system
   B   Followers were exempt from the religious tax (jizya)
   C   Its devotional practices made each Hindu strong
   D   It organized military resistance to the Muslims

6. Converts to Islam and Christianity found themselves
   A   Welcomed as equals
   B   At the same social level as before their conversion
   C   Still subject to the religious tax
   D   All of the above

7. When Shivaji offered his guru the kingdom, the guru
   A   Took over the kingdom and moved into the palace
   B   Told Shivaji to rule it in the name of Lord Rama
   C   Refused to accept it
   D   Divided the kingdom among his followers

8. Which of the following was NOT a hardship endured by Hindus during this period?
   A   The heavy religious tax
   B   The destruction of temples
   C   The powerful Bhakti Movement
   D   Being regarded as kafirs

9. Why did the British East India Company not encourage missionary efforts to convert Hindus?
   A   They found these efforts to be bad for business
   B   They considered Hindus to be 'People of the Book'
   C   They found the missionaries' methods unethical
   D   They thought Hinduism was a better religion

10. The game of Gyan Chaupar was intended to:
    A   Teach the path to spiritual liberation
    B   Be entertaining for children
    C   Convert Hindus to Christianity
    D   Show that going to heaven is not the goal of life

11. When did Hindus make and enjoy music?
    A   In formal concerts with musicians
    B   During their work day
    C   At the special events called kathas
    D   All of the above

12. What terms best describe Indian music?
    A   Improvisation
    B   Raga
    C   Tala
    D   All of the above

13. Which Indian art forms changed during Muslim times?
    A   Music and dance
    B   Painting and architecture
    C   Music and painting
    D   All of the above

14. Why did India remain mostly Hindu?
    A   The caste system
    B   Loyalty to the Hindu religion
    C   The personal nature of Bhakti worship
    D   All of the above

CHAPTER 4

India as Colony: 1850 to 1947

Mumbai's "Gateway of India," pictured here in 1924, was just started when King George V and Queen Mary arrived at this spot in 1911. The last British soldiers left through it in 1948.

MYERS BROTHERS

What You Will Learn...

The British Crown took over direct control of India from the East India Company in 1858. Economic exploitation increased. A determined and mostly nonviolent freedom movement emerged and finally succeeded, resulting in the formation of modern India and Muslim Pakistan in 1947.

British Rule's Mixed Blessings

What You Will Learn...

Main Ideas

1. India became a British colony following the 1857 uprising.
2. Under British rule, India suffered poverty, famine and lack of freedom. These inspired the Indian independence movement.
3. Through mostly non-violent means, India won independence after World War II, but Pakistan was divided off for Muslims.

The Big Idea

After ten centuries of alien occupation and a century of struggle, the Indian people regained their independence.

HINDUISM TODAY's Teaching Standards

This column in each of the three sections presents our subject outline for India and Hinduism from 1850 to 1947.

1. Assess the impact of colonization, especially English education, on the people of India.
2. Explain how the uprising against the East India Company led to the establishment of the British Raj.
3. Describe the history of India's movement for independence, including the role of Gandhi's nonviolent campaigns.

If YOU lived then...

You are a Hindu sepoy in the Indian army in 1857. New rifle cartridges have been issued. To use them, you have to bite off the tip, which is smeared with beef fat. You have never eaten or even tasted meat, as killing animals, especially cows, goes against your religious beliefs. If you refuse, you will be arrested—and possibly executed. If you run away, you risk the same fate. **What do you do, and why?**

> **BUILDING BACKGROUND:** Nationalism or patriotism is love and devotion to one's country. Before the 19th century, people felt loyalty to their regional ruler and culture. They were less concerned about the country they shared with others. Starting in the 19th century, people developed political sentiments for their country as a whole and promoted a national identity.

Understanding Colonialism

As we learned in the last lesson, the British East India Company came to dominate India through its clever use of political strategy, **intrigue** and military force. In 1858 India became a colony of the British Empire. Powerful nations, including England, Spain, Portugal, France and Holland, had used their financial and military power to establish colonies in Asia, Africa and the Americas. Many colonies, such as in North America and in Australia, were created by military conquest. The conquerors drove out or killed the native peoples, whom they regarded as subhuman. They then settled the land with immigrants from their own countries. Other colonies, such as India, were first opened through trade and commerce which eventually led to their foreign economic domination and political control. England's colonies included India, Burma, Ceylon, Malaysia, Singapore and hundreds of other territories large and small worldwide. The English defended their conquests by claiming that they were a superior race with a noble mission: to spread Western civilization. This sounds very racist today. But it was then a firm belief of most Englishmen.

While England profited from its colonies, the colonies suffered oppression and disease. In the 19th century, the British did bring notable advances of the Industrial Revolution to India. But a century of British rule drove a wealthy and vital India into poverty and weakness.

Britain introduced English education in 1835 to strengthen its power. Indians excelled in the new education system, with unintended results. They read, in English, how the American colonies banded together in 1776 to free themselves from Britain and establish a democracy. They learned how the French gained freedom by overthrowing their king in 1789. Indians rightly concluded that their ancient land—Bharat Mata, "Mother India"—had the same right as America and France to be free and independent. But it would take a century to achieve this goal.

The 1857 Revolt

The East India Company dominated India until the 1850s. A huge uprising in 1857 led to the direct and official takeover of India by the British government.

Many Indians were unhappy with the Company. It took over previously independent kingdoms within India. Its economic policies made most people poor. Its British-run police and law courts were inadequate or corrupt. Within their army, the British officers had little respect for their Indian soldiers or *sepoys*, and in some cases promoted their conversion to Christianity.

A relatively simple incident triggered the massive revolt. A new type of greased cartridge was issued for the sepoys' Enfield rifles. Word spread that the grease was beef and pork fat. To load a cartridge, one had to bite off the greased tip. The sepoys refused to use them: the Hindus because they considered the cow sacred; the Muslims because they considered the pig unclean. The sepoys **mutinied**, attacking and killing their British officers.

The revolt spread across North India, as Hindus and Muslims, elites and commoners,

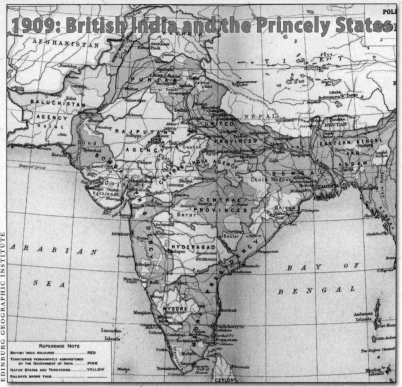

1909: British India and the Princely States

EDINBURGH GEOGRAPHIC INSTITUTE

REFERENCE NOTE
BRITISH INDIA COLOURED .... RED
TERRITORIES PERMANENTLY ADMINISTERED
BY THE GOVERNMENT OF INDIA ...... PINK
NATIVE STATES AND TERRITORIES ...... YELLOW
RAILWAYS SHOWN THUS

The red areas were under direct British control. The yellow areas, called "Princely States," had local Indian rulers who answered to the British.

joined forces against the British. Many landlords, left impoverished, joined the rebellion. Within a year, the British ruthlessly crushed the revolt, killing hundreds of thousands (some say millions) of soldiers and civilians.

Stories (some true, some false) of British women and children being killed by the rebels **inflamed** public opinion in England. Charles Dickens, author of *A Christmas Carol* and other famous stories, wrote that if he were commander-in-chief in India he would "strike that Oriental Race …proceeding, with merciful swiftness of execution, to blot it out of mankind and **raze** it off the face of the Earth." Although Dickens championed the poor in England and opposed slavery in America, he held a **rabidly** racist view of Indians.

The British were shocked by the uprising, which recalled the American Revolution. To protect their power, investment and income, they tightened their grip on the subcontinent by transferring rule from the East India Company to the British government.

ACADEMIC VOCABULARY

intrigue
secret planning to harm another

mutiny
a revolt by soldiers or sailors against their officers

inflame
to cause strong emotions

raze
to destroy completely

rabid
extreme or fanatical support of a belief

The British Raj

The new government of India was called the Raj, a Sanskrit word meaning to reign or rule. Its first steps were to ensure that no future rebellion would take place. The ratio of English soldiers in the army was greatly increased. Sepoys of various castes, religions and regions were assigned to separate units to prevent possible **conspiracy**. The population was disarmed. Ownership of guns was allowed by license only. Generally, Indians had no rights and no voice in their own rule.

The Raj expanded the rail and road system which allowed **duty-free** British products to be sold all over India. This, unfortunately, caused the collapse of major native industries such as cotton textiles.

Tax revenues from agriculture and industry that should have benefitted India instead went to England. Between 1770 and 1857, mismanagement worsened the effects of twelve major **famines** and many minor ones. According to official figures, 28 million Indians starved to death between 1854 and 1901. India's share of world income shrank from 22.6% in 1700 to 3.8% in 1952.

As early as the 1820s, many Indians wrote about the need to end British rule in India. The peaceful demand for freedom by nationalist political organizations continued decade after decade, at times turning into violent but unsuccessful uprisings.

The British improved India's legal, justice and civil service systems, introduced better military training, built a few universities and created telegraph, postal, rail and road networks. They did so primarily for their own political and economic gain, not to benefit the Indian people.

The Road to Independence

Mohandas K. Gandhi, born in 1869, is honored in India as the "father of the nation." After becoming a lawyer in England, he moved to South Africa. There he won political rights for Indian immigrants by nonviolent means. In 1915 he returned home to India and joined the freedom struggle.

On April 13, 1919, British General Dyer led an attack upon a peaceful political meeting of unarmed men, women and children at Jallianwala Bagh in Amritsar. In ten minutes, 400 people were shot dead and 1,200 seriously injured. Instead of being punished for his crime, Dyer was honored as a hero.

The **ruthless** massacre in Amritsar

Timeline: 1857 to 1947 ce

1860
First Indian indentured laborers arrive in South Africa; tens of thousands more eventually go to Africa, Fiji and the Caribbean

1869
Birth of Mohandas K. Gandhi who won India's independence by nonviolent means

Mahatma Gandhi

1876-1890
Fifty-volume *Sacred Books of the East* is published, English translations of Indian and other Eastern scriptures

1896
Lokmanya B. G. Tilak starts Ganesha and Shivaji festivals in Bombay to mobilize mass Indian nationalism

| 1860 | 1870 | 1880 | 1890 |

1857
British government suppresses widespread uprising and begins formal imperial rule of India

1863
Birth of Swami Vivekananda, India's first Hindu missionary to the West

Vivekananda

1876
Queen Victoria of England is proclaimed Empress of India

1885
Indian National Congress is founded to voice Indian concerns to the British government

1893
Swami Vivekananda represents Hinduism at the Parliament of the World's Religions in Chicago

convinced Gandhi that only a mass struggle against foreign rule would save India. From 1920 on, he led a national movement for freedom based on his philosophy of nonviolent resistance called *satyagraha*, "force of truth." Indian nationalists stopped cooperating with the government, refused to pay taxes and burned English goods in public. Gandhi and his followers were repeatedly beaten and jailed.

During the freedom movement, Hindus and Muslims disagreed about the democratic government they hoped to build. Muslims did not want to be a permanent minority in India and demanded their own country, an idea that Gandhi opposed.

World War II began in 1939 as Germany and Japan sought to add countries to their empires by force, just as Britain had done a century earlier. The war put Britain in the awkward position of defending its own freedom and democracy against Germany while continuing to deprive India of hers.

The Quit India movement was launched in 1942. Soon afterwards, Gandhi and other leaders were arrested. The movement became violent at some places, with hundreds shot and killed by police.

Britain's military force in India was composed of Indian soldiers and sailors commanded by British officers. By the 1940s, the loyalty of these hired servicemen to their foreign masters diminished as the demand for freedom swept over India. A 1946 mutiny by Indian sailors of the Royal Indian Navy convinced the British that it was only a matter of time before the entire military might revolt.

Crippled by World War II and nearly bankrupt, Britain gave up India and other colonies, including Burma and Ceylon. India's transition to freedom on August 15, 1947, brought with it a terrible tragedy. Pakistan was **partitioned** from India on the basis of religion. A huge relocation followed as 7.5 million Muslims moved to Pakistan from India and an equal number of Hindus and Sikhs fled Pakistan. A million died from hardship, attacks and riots. On January 30, 1948, a Hindu, enraged over the partition, assassinated Mahatma Gandhi.

Section 1 Assessment

REVIEWING IDEAS, TERMS AND PEOPLE

1. **Identify:** How did England justify its colonial empire? How did India fare as a British colony?
2. **Report:** What sparked the uprisings of 1857?
3. **Describe:** What changes did England impose as a result of these uprisings?
4. **Explain:** Why were there so many huge famines in India under the Raj?

FOCUS ON WRITING

5. **Analyze:** How did Gandhi and his followers fight for independence? Why did he choose to use nonviolent means?

B.G. Tilak

1910
B. G. Tilak declares, "Independence is our birthright"

1918
17 million people, 5% of India's population, die in Spanish flu pandemic; 50 million perish worldwide

Man of the Year

1930
Gandhi named Time Magazine "Man of the Year" as his fame grows in the West following the successful Salt March

1943
Three million Bengalis die in famine caused by British negligence

1910	1920	1930	1940

1900
India's population is 290 million, 18% of the world's people

1919
General Dyer orders troops to fire on an unarmed political gathering, killing hundreds; Gandhi begins noncooperation movement

1921
Subhash Chandra Bose advocates armed rebellion. In 1943 he forms the Indian National Army of 40,000 troops which fought against British troops in Burma.

1939
Beginning of World War II, which ultimately results in the death of 60 million people

1947
India gains independence. Pakistan is divided off along religious lines for Muslims.

The Challenge of Ideas

What You Will Learn...

Main Ideas

1. Missionaries and colonists believe that their culture is superior to all other cultures.
2. Swami Vivekananda popularized the Hindu belief that all religions are valid paths to God.
3. Gandhi's satyagraha campaign brought independence to India and inspired nonviolent movements for freedom and civil rights around the world.

The Big Idea

Hindu ideals of nonviolence and religious tolerance have helped shape today's world.

Key Terms

satyagraha, *p. 68*
colonized mind, *p. 69*

HINDUISM TODAY'S TEACHING STANDARDS

5. Describe the conflict of ideas between prominent Hindus, including Vivekananda and Gandhi, and British missionaries and colonists.

6. Identify the influence of Swami Vivekananda on modern ideas of religious tolerance.

7. Explain how the Hindu principles behind satyagraha have improved the lives of people around the world.

If YOU lived then...

It is May 4, 1963, Birmingham, Alabama, USA. A thousand students from the city's all-black high school join the nonviolent freedom protest led by Dr. Martin Luther King, Jr. to **desegregate** the city. Police knock them down using high-powered fire hoses and arrest hundreds. Your 17-year-old daughter is arrested and jailed for three days.

What do you say to her when she returns home?

BUILDING BACKGROUND: Dr. King went to India in 1959 to study Gandhi's methods. He adopted satyagraha, calling it "nonviolent direct action." King said it should so "dramatize an issue that it can no longer be ignored." Gandhi translated *satyagraha* as "truth force" or "soul force." Satyagraha, he taught, forbids inflicting violence on one's opponent.

Understanding the Power of Ideas

In the 19th century, India was fighting the British in a war of ideas. One battle was over religion: Christian missionaries believed it was their sacred duty to convert all Indians. Another was over colonialism: the British were ruling India by military force, supported by the idea that they were a superior race. Many thinkers and activists, key among them Swami Vivekananda and Mahatma Gandhi, challenged these ideas. Today nearly all colonies have been freed. Few countries, if any, would claim a moral right to colonize another. But religious conflict remains a crucial issue. Vivekananda's teaching of equal respect for all religions is more relevant today than ever before.

A Young Monk with a Message of Tolerance

The story of Swami Vivekananda (1863–1902) starts with a temple priest named Sri Ramakrishna (1836-1886) who lived near Calcutta. He was a mystic, a person who had visions of God and many profound spiritual experiences. Though not formally educated, he attracted followers from the city's prominent families. One was an 18-year-old college student named Narendranath Dutta.

When they first met, Narendra asked Ramakrishna why he believed in God. Ramakrishna replied, "Because I see Him just as I see you here, only in a much more intense sense." Narendra took

SWAMI VIVEKANANDA'S ADDRESS TO THE PARLIAMENT OF THE WORLD'S RELIGIONS

On September 11, 1893, Swami Vivekananda began his address with the words, "sisters and brothers of America," resulting in a two-minute standing ovation. He continued, "It fills my heart with joy unspeakable to rise in response to the warm and cordial welcome which you have given us. I thank you in the name of the millions and millions of Hindu people of all classes and sects.

"I am proud to belong to a religion which has taught the world both tolerance and universal acceptance. We believe not only in universal toleration, but we accept all religions to be true. I am proud to belong to a nation which has sheltered the persecuted and the refugees of all religions and all nations of the earth.

"I will quote to you, brethren, a few lines from a hymn which I remember to have repeated from my earliest boyhood, which is every day repeated by millions of human beings: 'As the different streams, having their sources in different places, all mingle their water in the sea, O Lord, so the different paths which men take through different tendencies, various though they appear, crooked or straight, all lead to Thee.'

"Sectarianism, bigotry and its horrible descendant, fanaticism, have possessed long this beautiful earth. It has filled the earth with violence, drenched it often with human blood, destroyed civilization and sent whole nations to despair. Had it not been for this horrible demon, human society would be far more advanced than it is now.

"But its time has come, and I fervently hope that the bell that tolled this morning in honor of this convention will be the death-knell to all persecutions with the sword or the pen, and to all uncharitable feelings between persons wending their way to the same goal."

RAMAKRISHNA MISSION

Ramakrishna as his guru and was trained by him for the next five years.

After Ramakrishna's death, Narendra took vows as a Hindu monk, becoming Swami Vivekananda. He gave up his further education and instead set off on **pilgrimage** across India. He deeply impressed many people in Madras. They raised money door to door to pay for his travel to America for the 1893 Parliament of the World's Religions.

At that interfaith congress in Chicago, the cultured and **eloquent** 30-year-old swami was well received. In his opening talk, he declared, "We believe not only in universal toleration, but we accept all religions to be true." The popularity of this Hindu message of respect and tolerance alarmed some Christian participants who had hoped the Parliament would prove their religion superior to others.

The *New York Herald* reported at the time, "Vivekananda is undoubtedly the greatest figure in the Parliament of Religions. After hearing him, we feel how foolish it is to send missionaries to this learned nation." Another reporter wrote, "The **impertinence** of sending half-educated **theological** students to instruct the wise and **erudite** Orientals was never brought home to an English-speaking audience more forcibly."

Vivekananda returned to India a hero. He aroused a new pride among Hindus and kindled in India's youth a nationalist spirit. Vivekananda founded the Ramakrishna Mission as a religious and educational institution to address India's social problems. He died on July 4, 1902, at age 39. Freedom fighter Subhash Chandra Bose aptly called Swami "the maker of modern India."

Vivekananda was not the first Indian religious and social reformer of the 19th century. Raja Ram Mohan Roy sought to counter the criticisms of Hinduism made by the British missionaries. He founded the Brahmo Samaj in 1828 as a new religion with Christian-style services. Swami Dayananda Saraswati was a Hindu traditionalist. He began the Arya Samaj in

ACADEMIC VOCABULARY

desegregate
allow equal access to public places for all races

pilgrimage
to travel to a sacred place for worship

eloquent
pleasant, fluent, convincing in speech

impertinence
lack of respect, rudeness

theological
having to do with the study of religious concepts

erudite
scholarly; having great learning

In 1930 Gandhi led a march to challenge laws that taxed salt and imposed burdens on the poor. His public spectacle of breaking the law by collecting salt at the sea was a turning point for the organized opposition to Britain's tyranny.

NATIONAL GANDHI MUSEUM

1875 to revive Vedic society and religion. He believed Hinduism could be purified by a return to the teachings and practices of the *Vedas*. Both the Brahmo Samaj and Arya Samaj encouraged Indians to be **egalitarian** and do more social service for the poor.

Vivekananda, on the other hand, had a powerful impact both on India and the West. In particular, he introduced the Hindu idea that all religions deserve respect as valid paths to God, an idea now firmly established in America. In 2008, polls found that while 76% of Americans identify themselves as Christian, 65% believe that "many paths other than my own can lead to eternal life." How different from Vivekananda's time, when most Americans were staunch Christians who believed theirs was the only way to God!

Satyagraha: Fighting without Violence

Mahatma Gandhi was a devout Hindu, a skilled lawyer and a master politician. His strategy to gain India's freedom was *satyagraha*, "truth force," the application of righteous and moral force in politics. Satyagraha is based on Hindu principles, including nonviolence, the ultimate goodness of the soul and a belief in the existence of God everywhere and in everyone. Satyagraha requires a core group of self-sacrificing and disciplined activists. To be successful, it must have widespread publicity, generating national concern and international pressure.

Since Gandhi's time, satyagraha has been used to win civil rights for blacks in America, improve conditions for California farm workers, end apartheid in South Africa and publicize human rights abuses in Myanmar.

Gandhi used the power of satyagraha to oppose the British salt tax to tighten its stranglehold on India's economy. The Raj imposed strict controls on salt production and a stiff tax on its sale. People could be arrested for making or selling salt. This **callous** tax on a basic necessity of life especially burdened the poor. To Gandhi, the salt tax symbolized the **tyranny** of the Raj.

Gandhi's dramatic revolt, the Salt March, began on March 12, 1930. Tens of thousands of people cheered as he walked 390 kilometers from his Sabarmati Ashram in Ahmedabad, Gujarat, to Dandi Beach. After morning prayers on April 6, he collected salt on the seashore and proclaimed, "With this, I am shaking the foundations of the British Empire." Hearing this, people all across India freely collected and sold salt. Tens of thousands were arrested, including 18,000 women. The march was closely covered by the international press, making Gandhi famous in Europe and America.

Six weeks later, hundreds of marchers attempted to take over the Dharasana Saltworks, 300 kilometers north of Bombay. The ensuing clash was reported worldwide by Webb Miller of United Press International: "Police charged [the marchers], swinging their clubs and **belaboring** the raiders on all sides. The volunteers made no resistance. As the police swung hastily with their sticks, the natives simply dropped in their tracks. Less than 100 yards away I could hear the dull impact of clubs against bodies. The watching crowds gasped, or sometimes cheered, as the volunteers crumpled before the police without even raising their arms to ward off the blows."

Professor Richard Johnson wrote, "It is widely believed that the Salt Campaign turned the tide in India. All the violence was committed by the British and their Indian soldiers. The legitimacy of the Raj was never reestablished for the majority of Indians and an ever increasing number of British subjects." The independence struggle was now truly a mass movement.

In a similar way, in 1963 Martin Luther King forced the desegregation of Birmingham, Alabama. **Civil rights** activists were arrested by the hundreds as they attempted to peacefully **integrate** the city's restaurants, shops and churches. Violent attacks by police on unarmed, nonresisting marchers attracted worldwide attention. The United States was shamed and embarrassed as a result. New laws were soon passed requiring equal rights for all.

The Colonized Mind

The nonviolent strategies of satyagraha helped Indians and black Americans attain freedom after centuries of domination. But decades later, they and their descendants still felt inferior to white people. This condition, called "the colonized mind," can persist long after physical freedom is won.

Many of India's colonized people, especially those educated in English schools, came to believe that everything about themselves was inferior to that of the British. Thus they considered English superior to any Indian language, English manners better than Indian manners, a suit and tie better than a kurta shirt and pants, and white skin better than brown skin.

Overcoming, or "decolonizing," the colonized mind requires a multicultural education, self-examination and rejection of externally created ideas of inferiority. The colonized mind is the most lasting negative impact of colonialism.

ACADEMIC VOCABULARY

belabor
to beat severely

civil rights
political and social freedom and equality

integrate
to end the separation of people by race

naive
innocent; lacking experience

Section 2 Assessment

REVIEWING IDEAS, TERMS AND PEOPLE

1. **Describe:** What did British missionaries and colonists believe about their culture compared to Indian culture?
2. **Interpret:** How did American journalists react to Swami Vivekananda's speech at the 1893 Chicago Parliament?
3. **Identify:** Where has Gandhi's strategy of satyagraha been used outside of India?
4. **Explain:** How did nonviolent protests "turn the tide" for Indian freedom and the American civil rights movement?

FOCUS ON WRITING

5. What Hindu ideals were promoted by Swami Vivekananda and Gandhi? How have they influenced today's world?

Eating: Indian Style

8. vege cocor

9. mango pickle

1. salt

10. fried okra with peppers

11. spi

The vegetarian meal at the right may look like a feast, but skilled *ammas* (mothers) prepare some variation of it every day for their families. This traditional South Indian spread is centered around rice. North Indians enjoy wheat-based flatbreads in place of or along with their rice, but the other dishes are similar. Lots of spices are used, including coriander, fenugreek, cumin, cayenne, cardamom, ginger, cloves, chili pepper, black pepper and cinnamon. Depending on the region, spicing may be mild to very hot.

The meal is served in several courses on a banana leaf freshly cut and washed or, more commonly today, on a round metal plate. After washing your hands, you proceed to eat with the fingers of your right hand by taking a small amount of one or two of the vegetable items, mixing them with some rice and popping them in your mouth. Seconds are automatic. In fact, you can only get the host to stop serving more food by covering the leaf with your hands. Water or a cool beverage, such as lassi (a salted or fruit-juice-sweetened yogurt drink), may be served at the end. When finished, you fold your leaf in half, top to bottom. In the villages, the leaves, complete with leftovers, are fed to appreciative cows. Nothing goes to waste, and no plates to wash! After the meal, water is brought for cleaning your hands.

Fingers, Forks and Chopsticks

There are three methods of eating in the world: with forks, with fingers and with chopsticks. Forks predominate in Europe, Australia and North America. Chopsticks are used in East Asia. Fingers are the most widespread eating implement, prevailing in India, Sri Lanka, Indonesia, the Middle East and much of Africa. Globally, fork-feeders are outnumbered more than two to one.

Chopsticks have a venerable history, dating back to 1200 BCE. Forks were introduced to Europe in the 11th century CE by a Byzantine princess who married an Italian. She outraged the Italians by refusing to eat with her hands. A Catholic priest pointed out that "God in his wisdom has provided man with natural forks—his fingers." The rest of Europe was slow to adopt forks. Many royalty, including Queen Elizabeth I and Louis XIV, used their fingers.

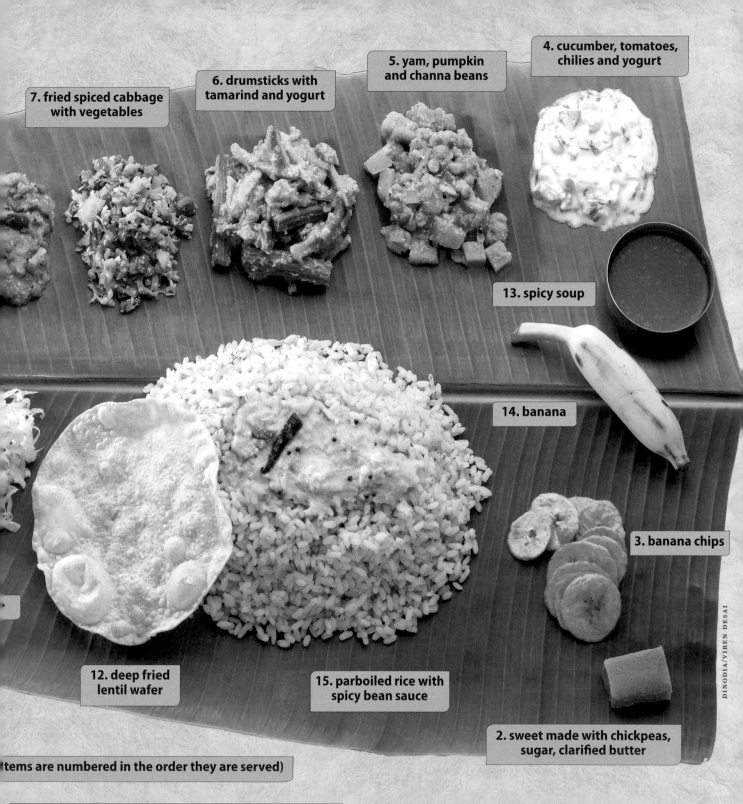

7. fried spiced cabbage with vegetables

6. drumsticks with tamarind and yogurt

5. yam, pumpkin and channa beans

4. cucumber, tomatoes, chilies and yogurt

13. spicy soup

14. banana

3. banana chips

12. deep fried lentil wafer

15. parboiled rice with spicy bean sauce

2. sweet made with chickpeas, sugar, clarified butter

(Items are numbered in the order they are served)

DINODIA/VIREN DESAI

Understanding Other Customs

1. **Compare:** After reading about a traditional South Indian lunch and looking at the images above, compare and contrast it with lunch in your own culture. How are your food and customs similar? How are they different?

2. **Evaluate:** How do you usually eat food: with fingers, chopsticks or forks? List some advantages and disadvantages of these different ways of eating.

Rites of Passage And Initiations

If YOU lived now...

You are a Hindu American woman who just graduated from the university. Your parents' marriage was arranged, but you swore you would find your own husband. Despite your objections, your parents have secretly found you the "perfect husband." You meet him, and, surprise, he does seem ideal—except that your parents found him instead of you!

What do you tell your parents?

> **BUILDING BACKGROUND:** In precolonial India, a bride brought wealth to her marriage, called *stree dhana* or "woman's wealth." Usually jewelry, this remained her personal property, to be passed on to her daughters. Dowry is a different custom in which the bride's family gives money to the groom. Demand for dowry became common among the upper castes in British times because of changes in land and inheritance laws.

The Sustaining Power of Hindu Tradition

Hinduism survived the centuries of Muslim and British rule on the strength of its philosophy and traditions. We have examined a number of these already, including scriptures, festivals, pilgrimages, temples, puja worship, art, music and dance. Festivals, in particular, are central to the religious, social and cultural life of a Hindu.

In this section, we study two more traditions important to Hindu life: rites of passage and initiation. Rites of passage are the social and religious ceremonies marking important stages in a person's life. These include naming a child, the attainment of puberty, marriage and funeral rites. In Hinduism, these rites are called samskaras, which means "to make perfect." Initiations, or *dikshas*, are given by a priest, teacher or guru to bring a person into a new level of education, religious practice and spiritual awareness.

The Rites of Childhood

The samskaras of childhood begin before birth with home rituals to ensure the well-being of the mother and her unborn child. The name-giving ceremony is usually held at home on the eleventh day after birth. A pleasant sounding name with a religious or moral meaning is chosen and the father whispers it in the baby's right ear.

Solid food is given to the baby by its father six months after birth in the first-feeding ritual. Head-shaving, symbolizing purity, is performed for both boys and girls at a temple, usually at the end of the first year. At age four, a ceremony marking the beginning of education is done in which children write their first letter in a tray of rice. Ear-piercing, for health and wealth, is performed for girls and boys between the first and eighth year. Girls are **adorned** with gold earrings, bangles and anklets; boys receive earrings and a gold chain.

The *upanayana*, or sacred thread ceremony, is the final ceremony of childhood. It marks the formal beginning of student life. Students begin religious instruction and secular education appropriate to their intended occupation. In artisan communities, a similar ceremony is held for boys to formally accept them into their family craft tradition.

The Coming of Age Ceremony

The community celebrates a girl's entrance into puberty with the *ritu kala* samskara, a home ceremony conducted by the family and close relatives. In the Tamil tradition of South India, for example, the girl bathes and then dresses in her first sari. The family invokes Goddess Lakshmi to bless the young woman with happiness and wealth. She is given many gifts, the first of which is always made of gold. Even today, this samskara is a major event for Hindu girls. It is a joyous time of gift-giving, yet serious as well. A vow of **chastity** until marriage may be taken at the same time.

The Rites of Marriage

Hindu weddings are conducted before a sacred fire. This practice dates back thousands of years to Vedic times. Agni, the God of Fire, is called to serve as divine witness to the marriage vows. Weddings are held in special halls. A Hindu wedding can be an elaborate affair spread out over several days attended by many hundreds of guests.

The wedding ceremony is performed by a priest, who invokes Agni by building a small fire in an open brick altar on the ground.

HONORING LIFE'S IMPORTANT MOMENTS

At left, a brother and sister both have the samskaras of head shaving and ear piercing (yes, it hurts) at a South Indian temple; at right a couple in Maharashtra State take seven steps around the sacred fire to complete their marriage ceremony

Below a funeral takes place at the cremation ghats along the Ganga River in the holy city of Varanasi.

(above) Wrapping a silk sari in *nivi* style: 1) the plain end is held at the right waist and the rest is passed around the back; 2) seven to twelve pleats are made; 3) the remaining material is passed around the back; 4) the decorative end is draped up and over the left shoulder. (below left) A Saivite does japa while visualizing Lord Siva; (below right) boys receive the sacred thread during the *upanayana* samskara.

A. MANIVEL

DINODIA

The elaborate rituals normally take hours. Close relatives are brought forward to participate and bless the couple. The groom puts *sindur*, red coloring, on the part in his bride's hair, indicating her new status as a married woman.

The final moment comes when the bride and groom take seven steps together around the fire to symbolize the journey of life they will take together. The first step is for strength, the second for health, the third for wealth, the fourth for happiness, the fifth for children, the sixth for a long marriage and the seventh for loyalty and everlasting friendship. The bride and groom usually go to a temple for blessings after the wedding.

Death and Cremation

When a person is close to death, relatives gather around. They sit for hours with him or her, singing religious songs, reading scripture and chanting prayers to create a spiritual environment and ease the loved-one's departure.

After death, the body is bathed and wrapped in white cloth, then taken to the cremation grounds and placed on a wood **pyre** which is lit by the eldest son. The funeral ceremony also requires Agni, God of Fire. He is called upon to consume the body. Cremation swiftly releases the soul from this incarnation and frees it for the next. The following day, the family collects the ashes, to be scattered later in a sacred river or other chosen place.

Home rituals honor the departed soul on the 10th and 13th days after death and yearly thereafter during the two-week period dedicated to honoring one's ancestors each fall. These rites help console loved ones and invite the soul to reincarnate back into the family in the future.

Religious Initiations

A mantra is a sacred word or phrase, usually in Sanskrit. Mantra *diksha* is the most common Hindu initiation. It authorizes the repetition of a mantra as a daily spiritual practice. "Aum Namo Narayanaya" is a mantra chanted in the Vaishnavite tradition. It means "Homage to Lord Vishnu." "Aum Namah

74 HISTORY OF HINDU INDIA

Sannyas diksha is the initiation that makes one a swami or *sannyasin*. A female swami is called a *swamini*. These **monastics** are spiritual leaders and examples for Hindus. This initiation is conducted by a guru after years of training and qualification.

Typically the rites include the shaving of the head, discarding all possessions and thereafter dressing in simple orange robes. In order to be closer to God, the initiate lets go of all worldly things: family life, career, worldly desires and personal ambition. The monastic takes lifetime vows proclaiming his spiritual goal of God Realization. Now born anew, he receives a new name. In some traditions, the initiate symbolically conducts his own funeral ceremony before the sacred fire. This symbolizes the death of his past and personal ego.

Many Hindu monks live in spiritual communities called ashrams. Others wander alone throughout India, begging for their food and spending no more than three days in one place. There are dozens of monastic orders in India, some with hundreds of thousands of monks.

> Young men, some born outside India, are initiated as swamis of the BAPS Swaminarayan Sanstha, November 4, 2005, in New Delhi

Sivaya" is of the Saivite tradition. At the high point of the sacred thread ceremony, students are initiated in a mantra prayer to the Sun God requesting Him to guide their thinking.

Japa is a form of meditation in which God is visualized while chanting a mantra, silently or aloud, 108 times. The repetitions are counted on a strand of sacred beads called a *mala*. Mantra initiation gives power to *japa*. One teacher explained, "Chanting a mantra without initiation is like writing a check without money in the bank."

Mantra *diksha* may be given as early as age six or later in life when a guru is chosen. After initiation, the devotee is obligated to perform *japa* each day as an important part of spiritual practice, called *sadhana*.

Vishesha diksha is initiation into personal daily worship called *puja*. It requires learning the rites, including chanting the prayers in Sanskrit, knowing the meaning of each part of the ritual and vowing to perform it each day in one's home shrine. This is a private worship, different from the public puja performed by priests in temples.

CHAPTER SUMMARY

The uprising of 1857 brought India under formal British imperial rule. Exploitation of the country continued. Mahatma Gandhi's efforts, the threat of revolt and changes in world affairs forced the British to free India in 1947. Before leaving, the British divided Pakistan from India along religious lines. The nation was left impoverished, through a new middle class had come into existence. Traditional religious beliefs and social practices were little changed by colonial rule.

ACADEMIC VOCABULARY

pyre
a pile of wood for burning a dead body

monastic
a monk or nun under religious vows

Section 3 Assessment

REVIEWING IDEAS, TERMS AND PEOPLE

1. **Define:** What is a rite of passage?
2. **Analyze:** Why do Hindus cremate their dead?
3. **Explain:** Why does an initiate to a monastic order perform his or her own funeral ceremony?
4. **Identify:** What Hindu ceremony must be performed before one can effectively practice japa?

FOCUS ON WRITING

5. **Apply:** How do you think these ceremonies helped Hinduism survive centuries of foreign rule?

Monuments to two saints—one ancient, one modern—proudly stand at India's southern tip

THOMAS KELLY

Two memorials stand on islands off the coast at India's southernmost point, Kanyakumari. On the opposite page is the Vivekananda Rock Memorial. In 1892, Swami Vivekananda, at the time a wandering monk, swam thousands of yards out to this island. After fasting and meditating there for three days, he had a vision of his life's mission. He saw how to overcome the terrible impact of British colonization on Hindu self-esteem. Above is the 133-foot-tall granite statue of a saint named Tiruvalluvar. He lived 2,000 years ago and wrote the *Tirukural*, a work of 1,330 couplets about religion, friendship, vegetarianism, moral living, business, government and even war.

Kanyakumari

THE STONE MASON'S ANCIENT ART

The Tiruvalluvar statue is made of 3,681 stones and weighs a total of 6.4 million kilos. It was built by 150 sculptors and laborers using carving techniques more than a thousand years old. They completed the work on January 1, 2000.

PHOTOS: THOMAS KELLY

❶ The chief architect lays out the statue's foundation after the granite rock of the small island has been leveled

❷ Using a massive chisel, workers shape a large granite stone weighing several tons

❺ Saint Tiruvalluvar's face is 19 feet high. Each stone was lifted into place with ropes and pulleys fixed to a scaffold of strong palm trees.

❻ Every worker, rock and piece of equipment had to be ferried to the small island by boat. In the 1999 photo above, the grand statue was nearly finished. Its total cost: 1.4 million US dollars.

③ Blacksmiths at the worksite manually sharpen steel chisels by the hundreds every day for the stone carvers

④ A stone mason puts finishing touches on one of the saint's enormous feet

HINDUISM'S PIONEER MONK TO THE WEST

In the early 1890s, Swami Vivekananda (right) wandered India without a penny to his name. He represented Hinduism at the Chicago Parliament of the World's Religions in 1893, where he gave a rousing speech about the glories of India. He was later welcomed by the rich and educated of America (below) and England as an extraordinary religious figure.

RAMAKRISHNA MISSION

RAMAKRISHNA MISSION

Honoring History's Great People

1. **List:** Name the large monuments to individuals you know of.
2. **Discuss:** What are a few reasons for building monuments to famous people?
3. **Explain:** Why do you think a poor monk from India was able to make such a dramatic impression on people in America and England?
4. **Analyze and Comment:** Who would you choose to honor with such a monument? Why?

DIRECTIONS: READ EACH QUESTION AND CIRCLE THE LETTER OF THE BEST RESPONSE

1. Countries justified colonies because they believed:
   A   Their people were superior to the natives
   B   They could offer a better civilization
   C   The natives were subhuman
   D   All of the above

2. What sparked the 1857 uprising?
   A   Corruption in the British courts and police
   B   Attempts to convert the sepoys to Islam
   C   Commanding the sepoys to use cartridges lubricated with beef and pork fat
   D   All of the above

3. From 1854 to 1901, how many Indians died in famines?
   A   6 million
   B   12 million
   C   28 million
   D   47 million

4. What happened to General Dyer?
   A   He was court-martialed and put in jail
   B   He was praised as a hero by the British
   C   He committed suicide
   D   He was quietly discharged from the army

5. Why did the Muslims want a separate country?
   A   They felt they could be more prosperous
   B   They did not want to be a minority in India
   C   The British insisted they move out of India
   D   World opinion favored the partition

6. What idea did Swami Vivekananda bring to the Parliament of the World's Religions in 1893?
   A   Only Hindus go to heaven
   B   Hindu religion is the world's only true faith
   C   Hindus respect all religions
   D   Hindus are seeking the respect of other faiths

7. How did Martin Luther King define satyagraha?
   A   "Truth force"
   B   "Passive resistance"
   C   "Civil disobedience"
   D   "Nonviolent direct action"

8. What was the main result of the Salt Satyagraha?
   A   The independence struggle became a mass movement
   B   The British police were punished
   C   The Raj apologized for the brutality
   D   All of the above

9. The term "colonized mind" refers to:
   A   A colonized people's sense of inferiority
   B   A psychological assessment of intelligence
   C   The advantages gained through English education
   D   The thinking of British Raj officials

10. To refuse more food during an Indian meal you should:
    A   Politely tell your host you have had enough
    B   Shake your head when approached with seconds
    C   Cover the banana leaf with both hands
    D   Quietly leave the dining area

11. A rite of passage is:
    A   A shortcut between two Indian villages
    B   A type of temple ritual held annually
    C   A ceremony that marks an important stage of life
    D   Arranging a marriage for a young adult

12. Mantra *diksha* is:
    A   A ceremony performed during a funeral
    B   An initiation to chant a particular mantra daily
    C   A type of mantra for Vaishnavites
    D   The daily performance of puja at home

13. At the *ritu kala* ceremony, a girl is given:
    A   A bath
    B   Her first sari
    C   Gold jewelry
    D   All of the above

14. At the initiation into *sannyas*, the monk
    A   Is given simple, orange robes
    B   Shaves his head and takes a new name
    C   Gives up all possessions
    D   All of the above

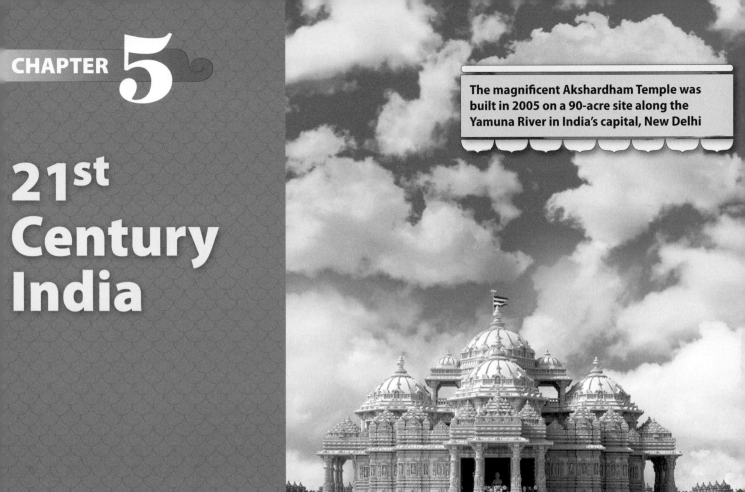

21st Century India

The magnificent Akshardham Temple was built in 2005 on a 90-acre site along the Yamuna River in India's capital, New Delhi

What You Will Learn...

India was suppressed by centuries of Muslim and British foreign rule. But after independence in 1947, its founders succeeded in welding together the ancient land into a strong, united, modern nation. The Hindu religion survived intact and thrives today in the world's largest democracy.

The World's Largest Democracy Is Born

Main Ideas

1. India's independence in 1947 was accompanied by the violent Partition.
2. India is a sovereign republic and is the largest democracy in the world.
3. States were formed largely along linguistic lines.
4. India has remained a voice for freedom and peace despite border wars with Pakistan and China.

The Big Idea

India is a unified, democratic, progressive nation with a strong central government.

HINDUISM TODAY'S Teaching Standards

This column in each of the three sections presents our subject outline for India and Hinduism from 1947 to the present.

1. Identify consequences of India's independence for the Indian people and for other colonized peoples.
2. Describe difficulties in unifying a nation with many distinct political and linguistic regions.
3. Describe the Indian constitution and political system.
4. Explain the causes and results of India's military conflicts since Independence.

If this were YOU...

It is 2004. Your family is part of a clan of blacksmiths who have lived in the same village for 1,000 years. You have learned the trade. But you did well in school and can go to college and take up a new profession. You would make more money, but would have to move to the city, breaking with tradition and leaving your parents alone in their old age.

Would you stay in your village or go to the city?

BUILDING BACKGROUND: From the first elections in 1951, every Indian citizen has had the right to vote, regardless of race, color, creed, gender or social standing. In 1913, Norway was the first country to allow all its citizens to vote. France only allowed women to vote in 1946. In the US, African Americans were not guaranteed voting rights until 1965.

Ending the Colonial Era

"At the stroke of the midnight hour, when the world sleeps, India will awake to life and freedom," proclaimed India's first prime minister, Jawaharlal Nehru, in India's Parliament on August 15, 1947. "A moment comes, which comes but rarely in history, when we step out from the old to the new, when an age ends, and when the soul of a nation, long suppressed, finds **utterance**." That moment set 370 million people free from two centuries of colonial rule.

Independence was accompanied by tragedy in the **Partition**. Pakistan was split off from India to form a Muslim-majority Islamic nation of 70 million people. West Pakistan lies adjacent to Afghanistan. East Pakistan, now Bangladesh, is at the mouth of the Ganga near Burma. Fifteen million people moved from Pakistan to India or vice versa in a dramatic and often violent population exchange. Over a million Hindus and Muslims died in riots and attacks that lasted months.

Newly free India led a worldwide movement to end colonialism. By 1954, Sri Lanka, Burma, Malaysia, Indonesia, and then Laos, Cambodia and Vietnam were freed. Independence soon came to Africa, once under near complete European domination. First Libya, in 1951, then Sudan, Tunisia, Morocco, Ghana, Guinea, Nigeria and so on. By the mid-1960s nearly all of Africa was liberated.

The Princely States

Newly independent India was diverse: 800 languages and dialects were spoken among 2,000 ethnic groups. Bringing unity to the ancient land after Partition was an amazing accomplishment by India's leaders.

Within India's borders were 17 provinces formerly under direct British rule and 562 virtually independent "princely states." These states were also granted independence in 1947. In theory, each could have become a new country. In practice, however, those within newly-formed Pakistan were expected to join it, and the rest to become part of India.

With Mahatma Gandhi's blessings, Sardar Vallabhbhai Patel took on the job of negotiating with the princely states. Patel contacted each prince or princess and explained the options: join India or stay independent. He then offered them all the time in the world to think about it—so goes the popular story—as long as he had their decision by that evening! The rulers had little choice. They had only held power because of British backing. The citizens of their realms were expecting the same freedoms as the rest of the country. In the end, the few who resisted were compelled to join.

The princely state of Jammu and Kashmir in northwest India was a different matter. Maharaja Hari Singh, the Hindu ruler of this Muslim-majority state, delayed in making a decision about which country to join until after independence. On October 22, 1947, militant Muslim tribals and Pakistani troops invaded the state. On October 26, Maharaj Singh agreed to join India. The Indian army was sent to defend Kashmir against the invaders, beginning the first of India's several indecisive wars with Pakistan.

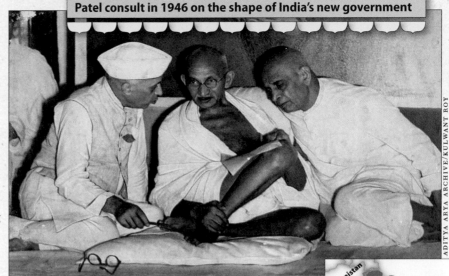

(left to right) Jawaharlal Nehru, Mahatma Gandhi and Sardar Patel consult in 1946 on the shape of India's new government

ADITYA ARYA ARCHIVE/KULWANT ROY

Partitioned India

India's Constitutional Structure

In 1947, a committee was formed to create India's constitution. It was headed by Dr. B.R. Ambedkar of the Mahar caste (an "Untouchable Community"), who was one of India's foremost legal scholars. The constitutional committee carefully studied the British, US and French governments, as well as traditional Indian political systems, choosing elements they felt were suitable for modern India. They unified the country by establishing a strong central government and setting a single pattern for state and local governments. They sought to ensure social equality and justice for every citizen.

The committee's draft was debated and revised over the next two years and finally adopted on November 26, 1949. At 400 pages, it is the longest national constitution in the world, because it includes many laws that in other countries were set by their legislature or courts after a constitution was adopted.

The preamble begins: "We, the people of India, having solemnly resolved to constitute India into a **sovereign**, **socialist**, **secular**, democratic republic and to secure to all its citizens: Justice, social, economic and political; Liberty of thought, expression, belief, faith and worship; Equality of status and of opportunity; and to promote among them all **Fraternity** assuring the dignity of the individual and the unity and integrity of the nation."

By comparison, the US constitution fits on four large pages, setting out only the spirit of the nation and the basic structure of the federal government. Individual US states have their own constitutions. India's constitution details the structure of government right down to the village *panchayat*, or ruling council. The powers and responsibilities of government are assigned either to the **Central Government** or to the state governments, or shared. Powers not specifically given to the states are kept by the Central Government. In contrast, in the US Constitution, powers not specifically given to the federal government are kept by the states.

At both central and state levels, India's government follows the British parliamentary system. The president is head of state, elected by the parliament. He or she serves for five years. The position is largely ceremonial, like that of the British **monarch**.

In India, elections are held every five years. The leader of the political party that commands a majority of seats in parliament becomes prime minister and forms a government with the approval of the president. If the party loses its majority, the "government falls" and new elections are called.

Establishing India's States

A key power of India's constitution permits the Central Government to merge or divide states as it sees fit. It used this power to reorganize the nation along **linguistic** lines. Areas where most of the people spoke the same language became one or more states. For example, the Tamil-speaking area of South India became Tamil Nadu. The Hindi-speaking region was split into several states. Having a single language made governing each state much easier. Today India has 28 states. It also has seven "Union Territories," which are ruled directly by the Central Government.

International Relations

India was a founder of the Non-Aligned Movement (NAM) of nations. These nations, mostly of Asia, Africa and Central and South America, sided with neither the US nor the Soviet Union during the decades-long "Cold War" after World War II. Prime

Timeline: 1947 to 2010

1947
India gains independence from the British Empire on August 15, after a long, mostly nonviolent struggle

1950
India's constitution goes into force on January 26, India's Republic Day

1950s
India launches land reform to redistribute to farmers hereditary holdings of large landowners

Ravi Shankar (at right) and George Harrison

1960s
Sitarist Ravi Shankar's tours in the West help popularize Indian music

1947 CE — **1950** — **1960**

1948
Gandhi is assassinated by a Hindu fanatic over payment of huge sums of money to Pakistan as agreed to at the time of Partition

1950
China occupies, then effectively colonizes Tibet; the Dalai Lama flees to India in 1959

1954
A.L. Basham publishes *The Wonder That Was India*—still one of the best histories of early India

1960s
Indian swamis begin coming to the West to teach meditation and hatha yoga

1962
Border war with China causes Ind to modernize and strengthen its military

Swami Chinmayananda

Minister Nehru was respected worldwide as one of NAM's strongest voices for peace and freedom.

But peace was a challenge on India's own borders. The hasty Partition left the subcontinent unstable. Pakistan's invasion of Kashmir in 1947 led to two years of open war with India. India's appeal to the UN resulted in a cease-fire. Since then, Kashmir has been divided by the "Line of Control," separating Pakistan-occupied territory from India's Kashmir. War broke out again in 1965 and also ended in stalemate. In 1989 Pakistan-backed Islamic **separatists** and infiltrators resumed violent attacks and riots. Since then, they have driven hundreds of thousands of Hindus out of Kashmir and worsened the security situation in the state.

In 1962 India lost a brief war with China over their disputed and ill-defined border in the Himalayas. The war was a deep personal shock to Nehru. He had taken at face value the Chinese government's promise not to attack, even when warned by members of NAM to not be so trusting. India was badly prepared to defend against the Chinese and had to appeal to the US for support, which was a humiliating compromise of NAM principles.

India's failure in the Chinese border war caused a complete rethinking of military strategy. Nehru's successors, especially his daughter Indira Gandhi, turned India into a major modern military power armed with missiles and nuclear weapons.

Bangladesh

Since independence, citizens in Bengali-speaking East Pakistan felt neglected by their rulers, who were mostly Urdu-speaking people based in West Pakistan. East Pakistan demanded economic and political **autonomy**. A nationalist upheaval followed. West Pakistan responded in 1971 by sending 100,000 troops to brutally put down what they regarded as an outright revolt. Civil war followed. Ten million refugees fled to India forcing India to come to East Pakistan's aid. In December, West Pakistan's forces surrendered to the Indian army. East Pakistan became the independent nation of Bangladesh, and the refugees returned.

Section 1 Assessment

REVIEWING IDEAS, TERMS AND PEOPLE

1. **Define:** What event in India's history is called the Partition? Why is it called the Partition?
2. **Explain:** How was Kashmir different from other states at independence? What has occurred as a result?
3. **Compare:** How does India's government differ from that of the US at the federal and state levels?
4. **Explain:** How did India reorganize its states? How did the strategy help improve state government?

FOCUS ON WRITING

5. **Analyze:** What was the Non-Aligned Movement? How was India involved in NAM?

1969
India becomes self-sufficient in food as its population reaches 500 million

1974
India explodes nuclear device in test at Pokhran

1990
300,000 Hindus flee Kashmir region as Muslim militants seek separation from India

1991
India begins economic reforms to loosen state management of its economy

1998
India develops a nuclear strike force

2010
US government report ranks India as the world's third most powerful nation

1970 — 1980 — 1990 — 2000

1971
East Pakistan declares independence as Bangladesh

1984
Indira Gandhi is assassinated by her Sikh bodyguards in revenge for army's attack on Sikh separatists in the Golden Temple

Indira Gandhi

2001
World's largest religious gathering ever: Kumbha Mela with 60 million pilgrims at Prayag, the confluence of Ganga and Yamuna rivers

Bathing at Kumbha Mela

Building a Unified Nation

What You Will Learn...

Main Ideas

1. India is a successful democracy.
2. The Indian nation carefully managed its economy for steady growth.
3. India is a secular country, but the various religions are not treated the same under the law.
4. Pilgrimage is a popular religious practice that helps unify India.

The Big Idea

India's unity and social and economic development have made it a major world power.

Key Terms

democracy, p. 86
secular, p. 88
pilgrimage, p. 89

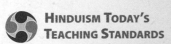

HINDUISM TODAY'S TEACHING STANDARDS

5. Discuss the elements that have kept India a unified nation.
6. Examine India's political, technological, economic, social and secular developments since 1947.
7. Explain the concept of pilgrimage and how it impacts the nation.

If this were YOU...

It is April 2010, and your parents have brought you to Haridwar from New York for the Kumbha Mela. You feel odd having to take a "bath" in the freezing Ganga surrounded by tens of thousands of strangers. But as you approach the river, those around you suddenly are like family. And after the bath, you are all talking together and laughing.

What creates such feelings among strangers?

BUILDING BACKGROUND: India's constitution provides for "reservations" for members of the lower castes and tribes—historically disadvantaged people. A quarter to half of the seats in higher educational institutions and the jobs in government are set aside for these groups. Without such quotas, many would not qualify for the school or job.

Planning for Progress

Newly independent India faced a host of problems—political, military, economic, social and religious. To maintain national unity, Nehru and the other great minds who oversaw the country's early years focused on running a good government. They had two key strategies: 1) to keep India democratic by ensuring that every citizen had the opportunity to be part of the political process; 2) to modernize the nation through educational, economic and social development.

The World's Largest Democracy

In all Indian general elections, the participation of the people has been enormous. Without a doubt, the democratic system has kept the country stable and united. But political parties quickly learned to win elections by creating "voting blocs," groups of people who always vote for the same party. A party seeks to convince a group that only it can truly serve the group's interests. Unfortunately, such appeals often run along narrow religious, **ethnic**, linguistic or caste lines. Issues that could otherwise be settled in a friendly manner are kept alive and used for political and occasionally **treacherous** ends.

There remains one internal threat to the democratic order: communist-inspired local uprisings in India's eastern states running from Bihar to Andhra Pradesh. Poor and tribal people support these

Pilgrim's India

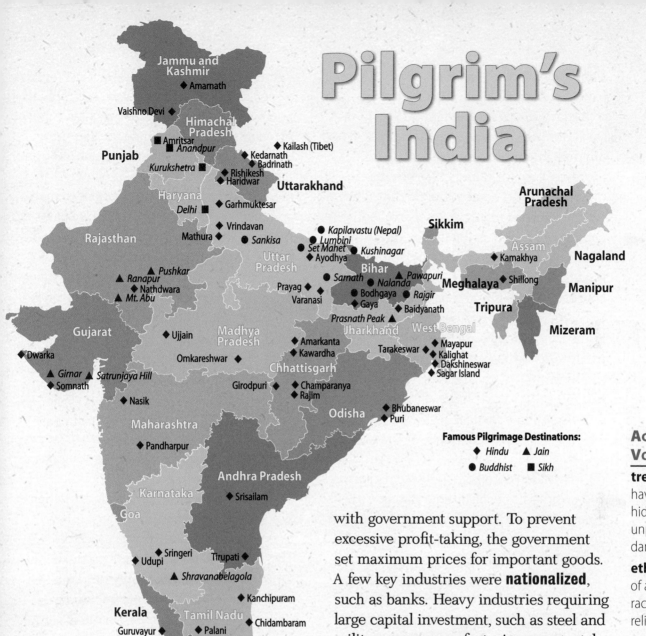

SHUTTERSTOCK

Jammu and Kashmir
◆ Amarnath
Vaishno Devi ◆
Himachal Pradesh
Punjab
■ Amritsar
■ Anandpur
Kurukshetra ■
Haryana
◆ Rishikesh
◆ Haridwar
Delhi ■
◆ Kailash (Tibet)
◆ Kedarnath
◆ Badrinath
Uttarakhand
◆ Garhmuktesar
◆ Vrindavan
Mathura ◆
● Sankisa
Rajasthan
● Kapilavastu (Nepal)
● Lumbini
● Set Mahet ● Kushinagar
Uttar Pradesh
● Ayodhya
Sikkim
Arunachal Pradesh
Assam
▲ Ranapur
◆ Pushkar
◆ Nathdwara
▲ Mt. Abu
● Sarnath
Prayag ◆
Varanasi
Bihar
● Nalanda
● Bodhgaya ● Rajgir
● Pawapuri
Meghalaya
◆ Kamakhya
◆ Shillong
Nagaland
Manipur
Gujarat
● Gaya
◆ Baidyanath
Prasnath Peak ▲
Tripura
Mizeram
◆ Dwarka
▲ Girnar ▲ Satrunjaya Hill
◆ Somnath
Ujjain ◆
Madhya Pradesh
Omkareshwar ◆
● Amarkanta
● Kawardha
Jharkhand
West Bengal
Tarakeswar ◆
◆ Mayapur
◆ Kalighat
Dakshineswar
◆ Sagar Island
◆ Nasik
Girodpuri ◆
Chhattisgarh
● Champaranya
◆ Rajim
Odisha
◆ Bhubaneswar
◆ Puri
Maharashtra
◆ Pandharpur
Andhra Pradesh
◆ Srisailam
Karnataka
Goa
◆ Sringeri
◆ Udupi
Tirupati ◆
▲ Shravanabelagola
◆ Kanchipuram
Kerala
Guruvayur
Tamil Nadu
◆ Palani
◆ Chidambaram
◆ Sabarimala
◆ Madurai
◆ Rameswaram
◆ Kanya Kumari

Famous Pilgrimage Destinations:
◆ *Hindu*   ▲ *Jain*
● *Buddhist*   ■ *Sikh*

armed separatist movements because they have seen little economic improvement in their region. Local police and government forces struggle to control these militant groups.

Economic Development

During India's first decades, the economy was a mixture of state control and free enterprise. Prime Minister Nehru began a series of "five-year plans," setting economic goals for agriculture, manufacturing, etc., to be met with government support. To prevent excessive profit-taking, the government set maximum prices for important goods. A few key industries were **nationalized**, such as banks. Heavy industries requiring large capital investment, such as steel and military arms manufacturing, were established and run by the government.

Overseas investment was regulated. India's years as a colony made her wary of letting foreign investors control any vital industry. **Import duties** were kept high, making it expensive to bring in foreign goods. India wanted to be self-sufficient and build its own economic **infrastructure** to meet the demands of its growing cities and villages.

A major issue was food. India was not producing enough to feed her ever-increasing population and had to import nearly ten million tons of food yearly from the US. The technological advancements of the

ACADEMIC VOCABULARY

treacherous
having hidden and unpredictable dangers

ethnic
of a specific place, race, culture or religious origin

nationalize
government takeover of a business, such as a bank or railroad

import duty
a tax on goods brought into the country

infrastructure
the basic facilities of a nation such as roads, dams, bridges, phone systems, airports, railways

For some Indian states, such as Kerala and Uttar Pradesh, the economic activity generated by pilgrimage is a significant percent of the state's total economy.

"Green Revolution" resulted in India's complete self-sufficiency in food by 1969.

India's growth for the first 30 years was slow, but the economy was stable and **urban** unemployment low. By the 1980s and 90s, however, the world had changed. International trade and cooperation had increased. Countries with totally state-controlled economies—such as the Soviet Union and China—started having serious problems. In 1991, the Soviet Union broke up into many countries. Seeing a similar threat to its own economy, India began easing restrictions on industries and encouraging private business, free trade and foreign investment.

The results were dramatic (see chart below). India's rate of growth went from a low 3.5% to a healthy 7.5%. Its middle class rose from less than 5% of the population in 1950 to more than 17% today. The middle class is projected to reach 40% in 2025. India has evolved into a major world power through scientific and technological advancement, development of industries and defense build-up.

Religious and Social Development

India today is 81% Hindu, 13.4% Muslim, 2.3% Christian and 1.9% Sikh. It has the third largest population of Muslims in the world—161 million, after Indonesia and Pakistan. Relations between religions are generally peaceful, especially at a personal level. However, several religious riots and attacks have occurred at great loss of life.

INDIA'S PROGRESS	1950	2010
Population (millions):	300	1,027
Life Expectancy (years):	30	61
Percent of World Income:	3.8%	6.3%
Annual Rate of Growth:	3.5%	7.5%
Living in Poverty:	50%	27%
Percent in Middle Class:	<5%	17%
Literacy Rate (adults over 15):	12%	68%
(15 to 24 years old):		82%

India's constitution proclaims the country a secular state. Yet India does not treat all religions the same, as other secular governments do. For example, Indian state governments seized management of Hindu temples and control their income, yet they allow other religions the freedom to manage their own places of worship, including mosques and churches. The resulting oddity is that Hindu temple priests are **virtually** government employees. In addition, the laws regarding inheritance, marriage, divorce, adoption and other family issues are different for Hindus, Muslims and Christians. (For legal purposes, the term *Hindu* is defined to include Sikhs, Jains and Buddhists—all religions founded in India.) In truly secular nations, all religions follow the same laws and freely manage their own religious property. The unequal treatment of religions in India is an ongoing source of conflict. It is ironic that Hinduism, the majority religion, has fewer rights than minority faiths.

The Power of Pilgrimage

One religious practice unites India as a nation: **pilgrimage**. There are hundreds of national pilgrimage destinations across India, and thousands at the regional level. The holy city of Varanasi welcomes 100,000 pilgrims a day, and a single temple, Tirupati, hosts 50,000 and more each day. Pilgrimage to religious sites is so popular that families plan their vacations around them. In India a vacation is not only for relaxation and fun; it is also a religious experience and opportunity for cultural interaction.

Throughout Indian history, the movement of pilgrims has had significant impact on the religious and cultural unity of the country. Pilgrims create a continuous religious conversation as they travel about the land. Religious discussions form a bond among travelers and promote a sense of belonging

PHOTOS: THOMAS KELLY

RAMESWARAM

The huge Rameswaram temple near the southern tip of India is a prime pilgrimage destination for Hindus of all sects. Here Lord Rama established a shrine to Siva upon Rama's successful rescue of his wife Sita in Lanka, as recorded in the *Ramayana*.

The central practice here is ritual bathing, a common practice at many pilgrimage destinations—Haridwar and Varanasi, for example. This doesn't mean bathing with soap, but immersing oneself fully clothed in a river or lake as a blessing. Ritual bathing is found in Buddhism, Judaism, Christianity, Islam and other religions. The bath-

ing may be full immersion, sprinkling or washing hands and feet.

At Rameswaram, there is not just one ritual bath, but 22, beginning in the nearby ocean. From that salty dip, you and your fellow pilgrims walk, completely soaked, to the temple. There a temple helper leads you to a courtyard inside the entrance where he drops a bucket 20 feet into the first well, pulls it back up by a rope and pours the holy water over your head. He then leads you rapidly, sometimes running, from well to well. You lose all sense of direction as you zig-zag through the stone corridors and courtyards of this ancient, **labyrinthine** temple. Despite the wells being so close together,

their waters are of different tastes and temperatures. According to temple **lore**, the water of each cleanses the pilgrim of a specific sin. Devout pilgrims hold a past transgression firmly in mind while being doused by each bucketful of water, which they believe cleanses them of that particular karma. Skeptics are present, naturally, even among pilgrims. But few depart the 22nd well without a feeling that something quite extraordinary and purifying has happened to them during those two hours.

to the country and religion. Such interactions are repeated at thousands of destinations each year.

The map on page seven shows the most important Hindu pilgrimage sites in India, as well as those significant to Jains, Buddhists and Sikhs. Prominent sites, such as Varanasi, Mathura, Ayodhya, Ujjain and Rameswaram, attract huge crowds year around. Most sites, however, are crowded with devotees only during annual festivals. For example, hundreds of thousands attend the summer festival at the Jagannath Temple in Puri, Odisha. Three huge chariots carrying the temple Deities are pulled through the streets by crowds tugging on ropes a foot in diameter. Similarly, devotees of Lord Krishna flock to the towns of Vrindavan and Mathura during Krishna Janmashtami and other major festivals.

Several pilgrimages require serious effort,

such as Amarnath Cave. It is located 12,700 feet high in the Himalayas, in Jammu and Kashmir. Every summer 400,000 pilgrims walk on a narrow, rocky trail for four or five days to reach this sacred shrine to Lord Siva.

Section 2 Assessment

REVIEWING IDEAS, TERMS AND PEOPLE

1. **Explain:** How did India's economy change in the 1990s? Why?
2. **Evaluate:** Is life for the average Indian better today than it was before independence? Provide several examples.
3. **Elaborate:** Why do you think family laws are different for Hindus, Christians and Muslims in India?
4. **Describe:** What do pilgrims do at Rameswaram temple? How does it affect their lives?

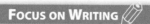

FOCUS ON WRITING

5. **Analyze:** How does the practice of pilgrimage help unify India's diverse peoples?

The Impact of Hindu Ideas Today

HINDUISM TODAY'S TEACHING STANDARDS

8. Define "soft" and "hard" power and apply these concepts to India.
9. Analyze the influence of Hindu metaphysics, theology, yoga and meditation in the Western world today.
10. Describe how Indian culture found its way to the West, including medicine, movies and food.

If this were YOU...

You have had a persistent cough for many months. A Western doctor has given you medicine to control the symptoms, but it won't cure the underlying illness. You go to an ayurvedic doctor, who prescribes certain healing herbs and a better diet. It is more work on your part, and it will take time for his remedy to make you well.

Do you try ayurveda or stay with your first doctor?

> **BUILDING BACKGROUND:** In this section we discuss India's "soft power" as opposed to its "hard power." Hard power is a nation's military and/or economic strength used to impact international affairs. Soft power refers to the influence of a nation's ideas, culture and values on the way others believe, think and act.

Dharma and the Future

In our modern world, Hindu ideas have spread far and wide from their origin in India. In Chapter Four (covering 1850 to 1947), we spoke of two of these ideas: respect for all religions and political change by nonviolent methods. In 2009, the Pew Forum on Religion and Public Life conducted a poll in which they asked Americans about their belief in a few "Eastern" concepts. The results showed that 24% believe in reincarnation, 23% in "yoga not just as exercise but as a spiritual practice" and 26% in "spiritual energy located in physical things like mountains, trees, crystals." This is nothing new: polls of Americans show similar numbers of believers, at least in reincarnation, as far back as the 1950s.

When did these ideas come to America? Many Native American tribes believe in reincarnation and spiritual energy located in physical things. While traveling in the American West in the 1890s, Swami Vivekananda was astonished to meet a cowboy who said he firmly believed in reincarnation. He may have learned the idea from the Native Americans, or perhaps discovered it on his own.

These spiritual concepts shared by many faiths throughout the world tend to be identified as Eastern or specifically Hindu, because it is within the Hindu tradition that they are logically and clearly explained and their **theological** foundations clarified. In this section we will explore how Hindu metaphysics (the study of reality beyond our five senses) came to the West. Hindu **theology**, **yoga**, meditation and **ayurveda** found a receptive audience.

Hindu Ideas Spread to the West

Hindu metaphysics arrived in America and Europe early in the 19th century in translations of Hindu scriptures—the *Vedas, Upanishads* and *Bhagavad Gita.* Scholars, writers and poets immediately found value in the concepts of karma, dharma, reincarnation and the divinity of the soul. They marveled at the Hindu concept of God as not only personal, but also immanent, (pervading all nature and humanity) and transcendent (beyond the physical universe).

America's 19th-century freethinkers deeply appreciated the Hindu openness to many religious paths and its freedom to choose one without condemning others as wrong. All these ideas are prominent in the writings of Ralph Waldo Emerson, Walt Whitman and Henry David Thoreau. They influenced generations of writers and scholars, notably Herman Melville, William James, T. S. Eliot, Aldous Huxley and Christopher Isherwood.

Hindu teachers first came to the West in the late 19th century. Many were prominent, but Swami Vivekananda (see Chapter Four) was by far the most influential. He and other swamis and yoga teachers were popular with the educated and artistic communities, including famous scholars and actors. In the 1940s and 50s, Swami Prabhavananda translated the *Bhagavad Gita* and *Upanishads* with the help of American devotees who were skilled writers. His clear and approachable books became popular, bringing these Hindu texts to millions in the West. Paramahansa Yogananda's classic *Autobiography of a Yogi,* published in 1946, introduced the idea of a life of spiritual striving and experience in story form.

The 1960s brought a wave of Hindu teachers to the West. Their teachings were eagerly welcomed by the youth of the **New Age**. Since then, karma, reincarnation and other Hindu ideas have become common in the songs, movies, art and novels of the West.

ACADEMIC VOCABULARY

theology
the systematic study of the nature of God and religious belief

yoga
"union," physical and mental practices intended to awaken spiritual qualities

ayurveda
India's ancient medical science

New Age
a Western spiritual movement drawing on Eastern thought

HOW HINDU THOUGHT AND PRACTICE CAME TO THE WEST

VEDANTA SOCIETY OF S. CALIF. ARCHIVES

TIME MAGAZINE

(Clockwise from above) Henry David Thoreau (1817-1862), writer and Transcendentalist philosopher; Swami Prabhavananda (1893-1976), translator of Hindu scripture; Swami Satchidananda (1914-2002), religious teacher and hatha yogi, addressing the famed Woodstock music festival in 1969; Maharishi Mahesh Yogi (1912-2008), teacher of Transcendental Meditation; B.K.S. Iyengar (born 1918), influential yoga master

Yoga

Central to Hindu ideas is the discipline of yoga. Hatha yoga, a system of physical postures, is the most widely recognized form of yoga in the West today. Generations of movie stars and dancers, back to the early 1900s, have helped publicize its benefits. In the West, hatha yoga is mostly promoted as a form of exercise in the West. But in India, it is part of a broader practice called *ashtanga yoga,* literally "eight-limbed yoga." Hatha yoga is the third of the eight limbs. The first two limbs are ethical ideals and religious practices, including nonviolence, chastity, honesty, piety and worship.

Hatha yoga poses have fun names such as downward dog, cobra, plough and lotus, which describe the shape the body takes in the position. Poses are done in series to quiet the mind and emotions and relax the body. To Hindus, hatha yoga is not just a form of exercise, but an essential preparation for meditation and development of spiritual consciousness.

Meditation

The fourth through eighth limbs of ashtanga yoga relate to meditation. The initial objective of meditation is to quiet the mind and emotions in order to move awareness to the higher chakras. This is done in part through hatha yoga, which calms the body, and in part through breath control, which calms the emotions and quiets the thinking mind. One breath control method is to breathe in nine counts, hold one count, breathe out nine counts, hold one count and repeat. After a while, you can do the counting on your heartbeat. The object of meditation is not to sit and just think, but to go beyond thinking into higher consciousness.

Ayurveda

India has one of the world's oldest systems of medicine, already described in Chapter One. Called ayurveda, "science of life," it is gaining popularity in the West. It is a **holistic** system which deals with the causes of disease, not just the symptoms. Ayurveda emphasizes a healthy diet, especially not overeating, and regular exercise and massage. It makes use of thousands of herbs, including common spices such as pepper, cinnamon and turmeric. Indian cooking uses the knowledge of ayurveda. The spices are used for their medicinal effects as well as for taste. A key practice of ayurvedic doctors is "pulse diagnosis," analyzing the patient's pulse to identify any imbalances or disease in the body.

Culture

India's Bollywood films, with their rhythmic dancing and singing, are popular worldwide. The word *Bollywood* mixes *Hollywood* with *Bombay* (now Mumbai), center of India's huge film industry. While they are not designed to promote religion or culture, these films convey the charming flair and flavor of Hindu lifestyles to people everywhere.

India is known for its varied and mostly vegetarian cuisine. It is commonly ranked among the top four, along with French, Chinese and Italian. The main ingredients of Indian cooking are rice, wheat flour, beans and a wide variety of vegetables and spices. Some Indian foods are notoriously hot, but most are mild. Indian restaurants abound in the West, especially in the UK, which has over 9,000!

DIANA KRAS/WWW.AYURVEDA4ALL.CO.UK

In ayurvedic pulse diagnosis the doctor doesn't just count the number of beats per minute. He feels for subtle variations in the pulse which give clues about the state of the patient's health.

GREETING THE SUN

1 2 3 4 5 6

7 8 9 10 11 12

DINODIA/VIREN DESAI

SURYA NAMASKARA

Hatha means "sun-moon" and is the name of the popular yoga exercises so common around the world. The name comes from the aim of balancing the male (the "sun" part) and female (the "moon" part) currents, mentioned in our next section on chakras. Each pose has a specific effect upon the nerve system. The most famous set of poses is Surya Namaskara—the Sun Salutation, or greeting the Sun God. It tunes mind and body, while being a good workout! In India you can see people alone or in groups performing Surya Namasksara to the rising Sun.

CHAPTER SUMMARY

Following independence, India rebuilt itself. It succeeded, improving its economy, halving the rate of poverty, doubling life expectancy and improving literacy six-fold. India is still a developing nation but is on track to be a superpower in the decades ahead.

India's heritage of spirituality and religious thought continues to dramatically influence the world, as it has for centuries. Scholar Stephen Cohen said, "India has become a global cultural superpower. Its soft power is second to none. Whether at the highest level of philosophy or the lower level of Bollywood, Indian culture is spreading."

Even in terms of hard power, India is already impressive. According to a 2010 report by the US government, India is today the third most powerful country in the world in terms of gross domestic product, defense spending, population and technology. The report says that as of 2010 the US holds 22% of global power, China 12% and India 8%. Japan, Russia and Brazil each hold less than 5%. By 2025, the report predicts, US power will decline to 18%, China's will rise to 16% and India's to 10%. The future of modern India appears bright as she overcomes centuries of suffering to resume her historic position as a leading nation in the world.

ACADEMIC VOCABULARY

holistic
based on the idea that the parts of a whole are interconnected

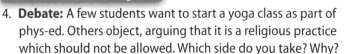

Section 3 Assessment

REVIEWING IDEAS, TERMS AND PEOPLE

1. **List:** What key Hindu concepts are popular in the West?
2. **Explain:** How did Hindu ideas come to America in the 19th and 20th centuries?
3. **Describe:** How do hatha yoga and meditation impact the body? What is the purpose of breath control?

FOCUS ON WRITING ✎

4. **Debate:** A few students want to start a yoga class as part of phys-ed. Others object, arguing that it is a religious practice which should not be allowed. Which side do you take? Why?

The Seven Chakras

Metaphysics is the inner scientific study of reality beyond our five senses. Many religions believe in the existence of the soul, heaven, God and God's love for man. These are metaphysical concepts because we cannot hear, see, smell, taste or touch any of them.

The system of chakras is a key metaphysical concept in Hinduism. The Sanskrit word *chakra* means "wheel." A chakra is a center of energy and **consciousness** in our spiritual body, or soul. There are seven chakras, located from the base of the spine up to the top of the head. Through the lower three chakras, we interact with the world of our five senses. Through the higher four chakras, we perceive and interact with the reality beyond our five senses—the world of metaphysics.

Great Hindu saints have seen and described these energy centers, though not all in the same way. According to Satguru Sivaya Subramuniyaswami (founder of HINDUISM TODAY), the seven chakras govern the faculties of: 1) memory; 2) reason; 3) willpower; 4) **direct cognition**; 5) divine love; 6) divine sight and 7) **enlightenment**. **Mystics** tell us that the chakras look like lotus flowers of different colors and numbers of petals.

The chakras are always active, but most people only experience the first three. As they evolve spiritually, they become aware of the higher ones. A great writer may use the fourth chakra's power of direct cognition. A person filled with love for all mankind is experiencing the fifth chakra. Someone seeing into the future through the power of divine sight is experiencing the sixth chakra. Through the seventh chakra, we can directly experience God and awaken miraculous powers.

Weaving through the chakras in the spiritual body are three *nadis*, or energy channels, which flow through the spine. The *ida nadi*, associated with the moon, is pink, emotional and feminine in nature. The *pingala nadi*, associated with the sun, is blue, logical and masculine in nature. Most women function mainly in the *ida* current. Most men function mainly in the *pingala* current. The yellow *sushumna nadi* is the channel of pure spiritual energy, flowing through the center of the spine. A highly spiritual person seeks to balance the *ida* and *pingala* and live in the pure energy of the *sushumna*.

Word Help

consciousness
thought, awareness, perception

direct cognition
knowing something immediately through intuition, rather than through the senses or reason

enlightenment
the highest human experience; realization of Divinity

mystic
a person who lives in the chakras of higher consciousness, seeking direct knowledge of God

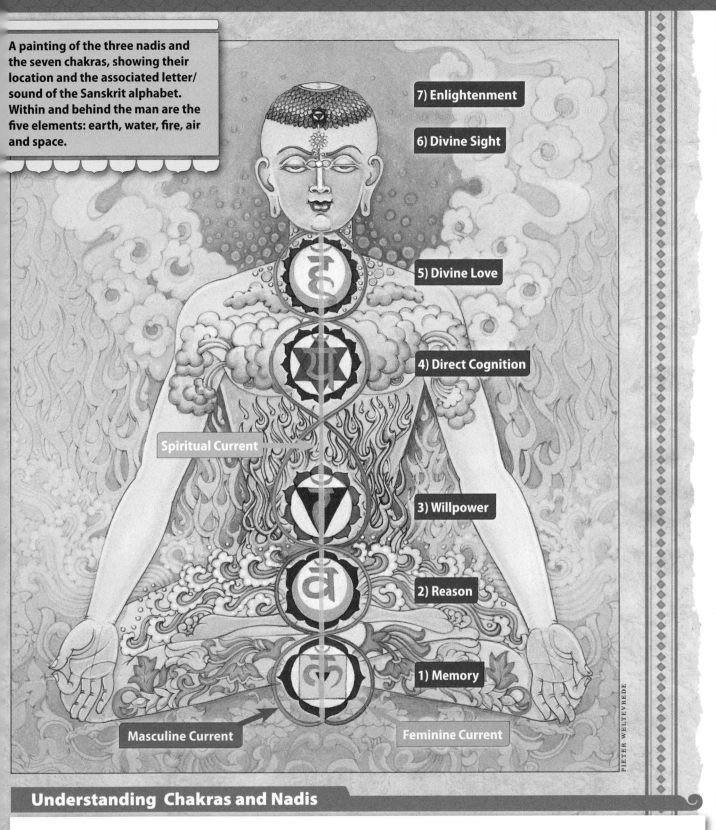

A painting of the three nadis and the seven chakras, showing their location and the associated letter/sound of the Sanskrit alphabet. Within and behind the man are the five elements: earth, water, fire, air and space.

7) Enlightenment

6) Divine Sight

5) Divine Love

4) Direct Cognition

Spiritual Current

3) Willpower

2) Reason

1) Memory

Masculine Current

Feminine Current

PIETER WELTEVREDE

Understanding Chakras and Nadis

1. **Discuss:** Is the belief in angels a metaphysical concept? What about UFOs? Examine beliefs such as global warming, hell, karma, reincarnation, the Golden Rule, evolution and freedom of speech. Which are metaphysical? Why?

2. **Analyze:** Review your day and assign your actions and thoughts to the appropriate chakra and nadi. What does this say about how you live and think?

3. **Explain:** Why do you think it is necessary to balance the masculine and feminine nadis to live in the pure spiritual current?

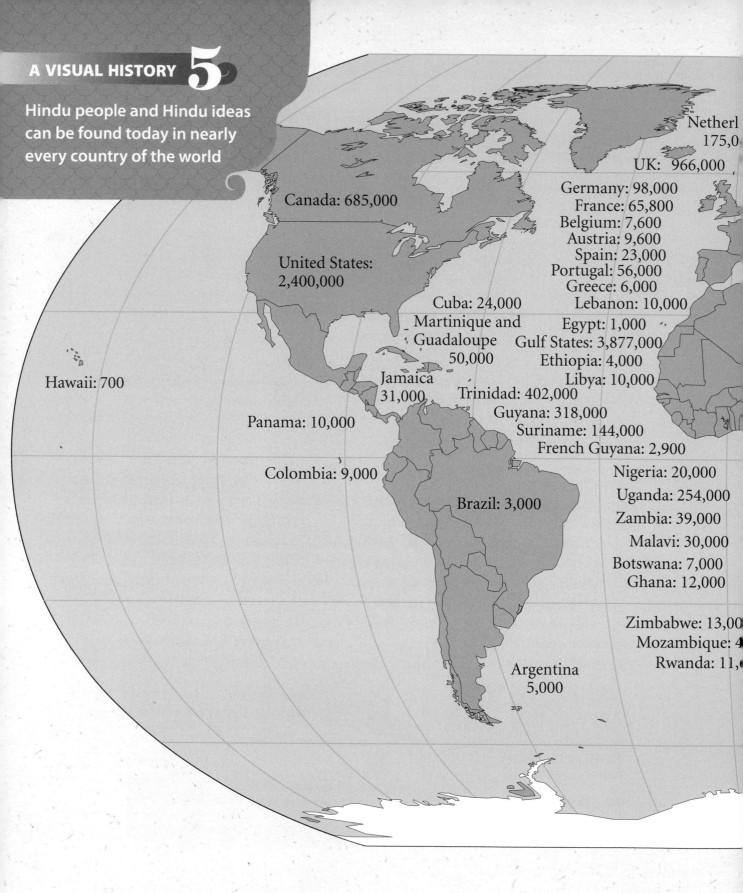

Hindu people and Hindu ideas can be found today in nearly every country of the world

Canada: 685,000

United States: 2,400,000

Hawaii: 700

Panama: 10,000

Colombia: 9,000

Cuba: 24,000

Martinique and Guadaloupe 50,000

Jamaica 31,000

Brazil: 3,000

Argentina 5,000

Netherl 175,0

UK: 966,000

Germany: 98,000
France: 65,800
Belgium: 7,600
Austria: 9,600
Spain: 23,000
Portugal: 56,000
Greece: 6,000
Lebanon: 10,000
Egypt: 1,000
Gulf States: 3,877,000
Ethiopia: 4,000
Libya: 10,000
Trinidad: 402,000
Guyana: 318,000
Suriname: 144,000
French Guyana: 2,900

Nigeria: 20,000
Uganda: 254,000
Zambia: 39,000
Malavi: 30,000
Botswana: 7,000
Ghana: 12,000

Zimbabwe: 13,00
Mozambique: 4
Rwanda: 11,

rway: 25,000
eden: 11,000

Slovakia: 5,400   Russia: 15,000
Denmark: 6,000
Switzerland: 30,000
Ukraine: 46,000
Uzbekistan: 3,000
Kazakhstan: 3,300   Hong Kong: 41,000
Iran: 15,000   Japan: 8,000
                                                     Bhutan: 167,000
Nepal: 23,000,000   Cambodia: 40,000

                                           Bangladesh: 15,800,000
Pakistan   Myanmar: 2,336,000
3,500,000   India   China: 16,000
                 974,000,000   Vietnam: 5,500
                                           Thailand: 68,000
Sri Lanka   Philippines:47,000
3,100,000   Indonesia: 5,200,000
Yemen: 157,000   Malaysia   Brunei: 6,000
Somalia: 2,900   1,737,000
Kenya: 386,000   Singapore   Fiji: 293,000
Tanzania: 389,000   203,000
Mauritius: 640,000
Reunion: 177,000   Australia:
                                  158,000
Madagascar: 20,700

South Africa: 805,000
Seychelles: 4,000

                                          New Zealand
                                            75,000

HINDUISM TODAY

WHERE ONE BILLION HINDUS LIVE: Hinduism originated in the Indian subcontinent—now the modern nations of India, Pakistan, Afghanistan, Bangladesh, Nepal and Sri Lanka. Most of the world's Hindus live in these countries today. A thousand years ago, Hinduism spread across Southeast Asia to Vietnam and the Indonesian islands. Then in the 19th century, Hindus were taken as workers to European colonies such as Trinidad, Guyana, Suriname, Reunion, Mauritius and South Africa. In modern times, Hindus have migrated to most countries of the world. Once settled, they have built temples for public worship to strengthen their religious life and express their faith.

Hindu philosophy teaches a deep tolerance and all-encompassing respect for other faiths. This attitude has a natural appeal in today's world, where people seek to live in peace with one another.

NEWSWEEK

WE ARE ALL HINDUS NOW
BY LISA MILLER

America is not a Christian nation. We are, it is true, a nation founded by Christians, and according to a 2008 survey, 76 percent of us continue to identify as Christian (still, that's the lowest percentage in American history). Of course, we are not a Hindu—or Muslim, or Jewish, or Wiccan—nation, either. A million-plus Hindus live in the way, the truth, and the life. No one comes to the father except through me."

Americans are no longer buying it. According to a 2008 Pew Forum survey, 65 percent of us believe that "many religions can lead to eternal life"—including 37 percent of white evangelicals, the group most likely to believe that salvation is theirs alone. Also, the number of people who seek spiritual truth ally believe that bodies and souls are sacred, that together they comprise the "self," and that at the end of time they will be reunited in the Resurrection. You need both, in other words, and you need them forever. Hindus believe no such thing. At death, the body burns on a pyre, while the spirit—where identity resides—escapes. In reincarnation, central to Hinduism,

ZUMAWIREWORLDPHOTOS

Lisa Miller's 2009 *Newsweek* article detailed America's shift to Hindu ideals, such as respect for all religions.

The Hindu practice of yoga is common in Western schools and many public centers for exercise, health and relaxation.

SIX KEY HINDU IDEAS FOR TODAY

1. Respect for all religions

"Truth is One, sages describe It by many names."
Rigveda, 1.164.46

2. The presence of God in everyone and everything

"God is, in truth, the whole universe: what was, what is and what beyond shall ever be. He is in all.
Krishna Yajur Veda, Shvetashvatara Upanishad 3.15-16

3. Ahimsa, doing no harm

"You must not use your God-given body for killing God's creatures, whether they are human, animal or whatever."
Yajur Veda 12.32

ART: S. RAJAM

4. Reverence for the environment

"The Earth is our mother, we are all Her children."
Atharva Veda 12:1:12

5. Karma, the result of our actions, returns to us

"Whatever deed he does, that he will reap."
Shukla Yajur Veda Brihadaranyaka Upanishad 4.4.5

6. Life's purpose is God Realization

"Lead me from unreality to reality. Lead me from darkness to light. Lead me from death to immortality."
Sukla Yajur Veda Brihadaranyaka Upanishad 1.3.28

Delegates from 60 nations at the 1988 Global Forum in Oxford, England, discussed the future of our planet. The contributions of the Eastern religions, including Hinduism and Buddhism, were given equal importance with those of the West.

Your Majesty and Mr. President, Meet Hinduism

In 2002, England's Queen Elizabeth II was greeted by the priests of Highgate Hill Murugan Temple in London in the first-ever royal visit of a monarch to a Hindu temple. (right) In 2010, Barack Obama became the first US president to personally celebrate Diwali in the White House.

Examining Hinduism Today

1. **Discuss:** What is important about a political leader visiting a religious place or celebrating a religious festival?
2. **Discuss:** What is the difference between respecting another religion and tolerating it?
3. **Explore:** How do other religions express the concepts in our list of six key Hindu ideas? Which ideas would be acceptable to people with no religion?
4. **Analyze and Defend:** What role do you think religion should play in today's world?

CHAPTER 5

Standards Assessment

DIRECTIONS: READ EACH QUESTION AND CIRCLE THE LETTER OF THE BEST RESPONSE

1. Which were consequences of the Partition?
   A   Pakistan attacked Kashmir
   B   15 million people moved to or from Pakistan
   C   One million people died in riots and from hardships
   D   All of the above

2. How were the states of India reorganized?
   A   Following the boundaries of the princely states
   B   On the basis of population
   C   On the basis of linguistic groups
   D   Along important rivers and mountain ranges

3. A state has what powers in the Indian political system?
   A   Only those specified in the national constitution
   B   All those not granted to the Central Government
   C   The same powers it had as a princely state
   D   Those granted by its state constitution

4. What did India's early leaders emphasize?
   A   Making every citizen part of the political process
   B   Achieving national economic self-sufficiency
   C   Guaranteed higher education opportunities and jobs for lower castes and tribes
   D   All of the above

5. How did India change its economic policies in the 1990s?
   A   Raised import duties on foreign goods
   B   Eased restrictions on industries and encouraged private business and foreign investment
   C   Became self-sufficient in food which made it possible to spend those funds within the country
   D   Invested in foreign markets

6. How has the poverty rate in India changed since 1947?
   A   From 50% to 10%
   B   From 50% to 25%
   C   From 50% to 40%
   D   Not at all

7. What is one way India's secularism is unlike the West's?
   A   State governments control Hindu temples
   B   Government officials must belong to one religion
   C   Only members of some religions can vote
   D   State governments control all religious sites

8. What unites India as one religious landscape?
   A   Control by one denomination of Hinduism
   B   Pilgrimage destinations throughout the country
   C   Everyone speaks the same language
   D   Everyone is of the same ethnic group

9. What is the purpose of bathing at Rameswaram's wells?
   A   To find release from past misdeeds
   B   To guarantee entry to heaven
   C   To be entered into the Hindu faith
   D   To cleanse the body

10. Which of the following is not governed by a chakra?
   A   Divine sight
   B   Willpower
   C   Sushumna nadi
   D   Memory

11. Soft power is defined as:
   A   Spiritual energy and force
   B   Economic influence
   C   Diplomacy
   D   Cultural influence

12. What fraction of Americans believe in reincarnation?
   A   one-sixteenth
   B   one-eighth
   C   one-quarter
   D   one-half

13. What spiritual leader brought Hindu ideas to the West?
   A   Swami Prabhavananda
   B   Maharishi Mahesh Yogi
   C   B.K.S. Iyengar
   D   All of the above

14. How does India rank in power among the world's nations?
   A   Second
   B   Third
   C   Fourth
   D   Sixth

Five Hindu festivals!

H INDUISM IS CELEBRATORY BY NATURE. Hindus miss no opportunity to set mundane matters aside and join with family, friends, neighbors and strangers alike to feast and have fun, to renew the home and the heart and, most importantly, draw nearer to God.

Festivals are perhaps more impressive and varied in Hinduism than in any other religion. The devout Hindu knows these are times of profound mysticism, when God and the Gods touch our world, revitalize our souls, lighten karmas and bless our families.

Yet festivals do even more than this: they are essential to the perpetuation of religion, periodically reigniting the spark of zeal and devotion in the community. They provide the spiritual public square where Hindus engage with one another, affirming shared values and enjoying life's intersections.

Before each celebration, vows are taken, scriptures are studied, pilgrimages are trodden and fasts observed in preparation—all individual acts of intimate devotion that bring the devotee closer to the Gods and keep him on the path to his inmost Self. As each festival begins, solitary adoration becomes a collective ritual, with millions of people taking their places in an ad-hoc choreography. Tradition is followed but the result is never the same; every festival is special and unforgettable in its own way.

Thus the Hindu is reminded of his faith

by the sounds, scents and the wild medley of tastes laid out for the feast. His mind and emotions are imbued with Hinduism as sacred mantra prayers are intoned, the spiritual teachings are recounted by saints and the Gods are praised in melodious bhajans.

Each state of India, indeed each village, lends a little of its unique culture to how a festival is celebrated, creating almost endless variations. But recently, with the growing Hindu population outside of India, festivals have acquired an international dimension. They provide a window into Hinduism for the non-Hindu populations in countries as far flung as Norway, Chile and Canada. At the same time, for Hindus immersed in foreign and often very alien cultures, festivals are the most visible and memorable sign of their heritage. Celebrated with unmatched fervor but with paced regularity, festivals serve as a reminder of one's identity and allegiance to Hindu traditions and ideals.

Ganesha Chaturthi
Honoring the Lord of Beginnings

During Ganesha Chaturthi, a ten-day festival in August/September, elaborate puja ceremonies are held in Hindu temples around the world honoring Ganesha, the benevolent, elephant-faced Lord of Obstacles. In millions of home shrines, worship is also offered to a clay image of Ganesha that the family makes or obtains. At the end of ten days, Hindus join in a grand parade, called *visarjana* in Sanskrit, to a river, temple tank, lake or seashore, where His image is ceremonially immersed, symbolizing Ganesha's merging into universal consciousness.

Who is Ganesha?
Perennially happy, playful, unperturbed and wise, this rotund Deity removes obstacles to good endeavors and obstructs negative ventures, thus guiding and protecting the lives of devotees. He is the patron of art and science, the God inhabiting all entryways, the gatekeeper who blesses all beginnings. When initiating anything—whether learning, business, weddings, travel, building and more—Hindus seek His grace for success. He is undoubtedly the most endearing, popular and widely worshiped of all the Hindu Deities. Ganesha Chaturthi (also called Vinayaka Chaturthi) falls on the fourth day in the waxing fortnight of the month of Bhadrapada in the sacred Hindu lunar calendar, which translates to a certain day in August-September. It is essentially a birthday celebrating Ganesha's divine appearance.

What do people do on Ganesha Chaturthi?
Devotees often fashion or purchase a Ganesha statue out of unbaked clay. Many sculpt Him out of a special mixture of turmeric, sandalwood paste, cow-dung, soil from an anthill and palm sugar. The Deity image

SHANA DRESSLER

SOUMYA SITARAMAN

Modaka Sweets

These rich, deep fried, fluffy, sweet dollops are the Mangalorean equivalent of the Tamil *kollukattai*. It is the all-time favorite of Lord Ganesha, who is described as Modaka Hasta, one with the modaka in His hand.

Preparation time: 10 minutes.
Cooking time: 30 minutes
Makes 20 pieces
Cooking equipment: A wok or deep saucepan, a perforated ladle, a lined colander to drain excess oil, a mixing bowl and serving plate.

Ingredients
4 cups thin beaten rice (poha);
1 cup semolina (rava) flour, 1 cup rice flour, 1 cup slightly over-ripe bananas, mashed, 1 cup powdered jaggery (or brown sugar), 1/8 tsp salt
oil to deep fry

Method
1. Mix all the ingredients together except the oil.
2. Add a little water and knead the mixture gently into a thick paste.
3. Heat the oil in the wok.
4. Drop tablespoonfuls of the batter into moderately hot oil and fry till rich brown. Drain and cool, then enjoy!

---

is placed in the home shrine amongst traditional decorations. A rite of worship and prayer, called puja, is conducted daily, invoking the energies of the Deity and inviting Him to reside in the clay image. Mantras are chanted and offerings are made throughout the puja, including incense, lighted lamps, cooked food *(naivedya)*, fruits, durva grass, tulasi and pomegranate leaves—and flowers, especially red ones. After ten days, a simple puja is performed before the statue is taken for a formal departure *(visarjana)*. Often entire communities, from dozens to tens of thousands of devotees, gather each year for this final day of ceremony. The icons are carried on an ornate metal tray—larger images are borne on a palanquin by several strong men—to a lake, a river or the sea. There Ganesha is consigned to the water after removing non-degradable paraphernalia.

What foods are offered?
Sumptuous foods are specially prepared for Ganesha, keeping in mind His elephantine nature and prodigious appetite. People offer several varieties of fruits such as mangos, bananas and sugarcane. Sweets are the elephant-headed Deity's delight, so to express their love families take great pains to make special tasty treats. Each family has its recipes.

Tidbits About Ganesha

Where is this festival most popular? Nowhere is Ganesha Chaturthi observed with more creativity and enthusiasm than in Mumbai, India. The city virtually shuts down as millions of Hindus celebrate.

Why is He worshiped first? Lord Brahma declared that any worship conducted without seeking Ganesha's blessings would be fruitless. He is considered a loving, playful, protective Deity whose blessings would grace any endeavor. He is therefore ceremonially invoked before weddings, housewarmings, taking an important exam, starting a new business and other important events.

What is His mystical work? Lord Ganesha is the God Hindus pray to when changes occur in their lives as they move from old established patterns into new ones. He is always there to steady the minds of devotees and open the proper doors as they evolve and progress.

What makes Him distinctive? Aside from His unique and endearing elephant head, Ganesha carries an elephant goad to prod us along the right path. He holds a noose to lasso foes of dharma and to draw devotees close when they venture off the spiritual path. His mount is a mouse. His big belly is said to contain the fullness of the cosmos. In His hand is a modaka, fruit or other sweet, symbolic of enlightened attainments.

Fact & Fiction

FACT: There is not just one path to God Realization in Hinduism, but many. Tens of thousands of distinct teaching lineages prescribe varying combinations of prayer, rites and rituals, meditation, chanting and the many yogas to guide followers in their spiritual evolution.

FICTION: Many wrongly believe that Hindus worship cows. Hindus don't worship cows. They respect, honor and adore the cow. By honoring this gentle animal, who gives more than she takes, Hindus honor all creatures.

Navaratri
Dedicating 9 Nights to the Goddess

Millions of Hindu women consider Navaratri the year's central festival, the one they most deeply connect to. These nine days dedicated to Shakti, the Goddess, provide an opportunity to seek blessings and commune with their own divinity. It is a time for sacred gatherings, austerities, selfless acts and intimate prayers. But Navaratri is not just for the ladies; everyone turns out for the joyous worship, festivities, plays, feasting and dance—all venerating God as the loving Mother Spirit that gives life to everything.

What do Hindus do for Navaratri?

Navaratri starts on the new moon of September/October. On the first day, it is customary to plant seeds in a clay pot which will sprout over the next nine days. In some communities, women prepare a specially decorated *kalasha*, a vessel symbolizing the fertile womb, representing the Goddess. Especially in cities in Tamil Nadu, families create elaborate shelf displays, called *kolu*, of handmade clay dolls. Adding new dolls each year and handing the collection down to the next generation results in some grand displays.

How is Navaratri observed in homes?

Each night, the Goddess "holds court," and special food offerings are presented as prayers eulogizing Her powers are chanted. Guests are invited to showcase their artistic skills, and all enjoy sweets and other treats. Women dress up and visit female friends and relatives, taking a tray of offerings which includes the betel leaf and nut that bear the gravity of a formal contract of friendship and loyalty. Other items on the tray—beauty accessories, fresh turmeric root and coconut—symbolize goodwill and fertility. They fast, pray morning and evening, and give food and cooking pots to the poor. Some families formally honor a prepubescent girl each day, giving her new clothes, treating her to a sumptuous lunch, and pampering her, affirming her femininity and affinity with the Goddess.

How are Shakti's forms worshiped?

In South India the first three days are dedicated to Goddess Durga, the fierce Mother who decimates negative forces. For the next three days, Lakshmi, the Goddess of prosperity, is revered. The last three days are dedicated to Sarasvati, the Goddess of learning and wisdom. In this way, Hindus honor women as the protectors of the family, extol their powers of fertility and endurance, venerate them as the source of good fortune and revere them as repositories of culture and learning. In North India one of the nine aspects of Durga is venerated each day. These nine days are celebrated by communities in East India as Durga Puja, treating the Goddess as the Daughter who has come to her maternal home for an annual visit.

What is the final day?

Vijaya Dashami, "triumphant tenth day," celebrates Durga's legendary victory over Mahishasura, a powerful being fraught with ignorance and selfishness. On the same day many celebrate Rama's victory over the evil Ravana. The celebration is a reminder to persist in the challenges we face in life. Local traditions vary widely, and this day is known by other names, including Dussehra, Dasara and Dashain.

SOUMYA SITARAMAN

Tidbits About Navaratri

What special events occur on Maha Navami, the ninth day? Books, musical instruments, equipment and tools are placed before Goddess Sarasvati for blessings, seeking Her gifts of talent, ability and inspiration. This rite, called Ayudha (weapon or tool) Puja, began when the kings of ancient India had their weapons blessed. Today any tool of one's trade may be consecrated: craftsmen's tools, books, offices, vehicles, computers, even iPhones! Devotees reflect on their skills, strengths, goals and needs. A key rite of passage for children ages three to five is performed on this day. Called *vidyarambha*, "beginning of learning," it marks the start of a child's formal education.

Are there group festivities? In the evenings, devotees gather to dance in halls and public squares. The Garba, Gujarat's popular folk dance, is a vigorous dance performed in circles while twirling, jumping, flailing the arms, clapping rhythmically and stepping in sync. In the Dandiya-Ras, sticks are part of the choreography. Dancing is a community expression of joy and togetherness.

Sundal

This is a high-protein, low-oil dish made from steamed or boiled whole chickpeas.

Preparation time: Approx. 1 hour
Serves: 6
Equipment: A pressure cooker, a ladle, a wok or saucepan and a dish

Ingredients

1 cup chickpeas, ½ tsp turmeric powder, 3 tbsp to ½ cup grated coconut, 1 tsp black mustard seeds, broken dried red chillies (to taste), ½ tsp asafoetida powder, sliced green chillies (optional), curry leaves, salt

Method

1. Beforehand, soak the chickpeas for 12 hours. Cook with the turmeric powder and salt in a pressure cooker (1:2 ratio of beans to water) until soft but firm, not mushy. Drain and set aside.
2. Heat ghee; add the mustard seeds and let them pop.
3. Add the curry leaves, chillies and asafoetida; roast the mixture slightly.
4. Add the cooked chickpeas. Stir gently over a low flame, taking care not to mash them.
5. Add grated coconut and salt to taste. Mix well.
6. Enjoy!

Hinduism: Fact & Fiction

FACT: Hindus place high value on self improvement through education and learning of all kinds. In bygone days women and men were educated from age seven: students lived as part of their teacher's family. Hindus revere women as the guardians of culture, family, religion, learning and prosperity. Modern Hindu society has the highest number of female spiritual leaders in the world.

FICTION: Many wrongly believe that Hindu women are prohibited from learning, performing rites, ritual and prayer. Hindu women are not oppressed or considered unequal to men, but honored and respected. Hinduism is the only major religion to honor God's feminine power!

Diwali
Celebrating the Triumph of Goodness

I f you rolled a bit of Christmas, New Year's Eve and the Fourth of July all into one, then catered the affair with mountains of sweets and savory snacks, you would have a taste of what it means to celebrate Diwali, India's best-known festival. It is a day of Hindu solidarity, when all Hindus gather in love and trust. It is observed by lighting rows of oil lamps and exchanging greeting cards, clothing and other gifts. Family bonds are strengthened and forgiveness sought. For many, Diwali marks the beginning of the new year. Joyous festivities and parties abound.

What occurs on Diwali?

Diwali (or Deepavali, "row of lights") is celebrated by Hindus worldwide to commemorate the triumph of good over evil, knowledge over ignorance, hope over despair. Oil-wick lamps are lit in every household, along with colorful strings of electric lights, causing the home, village and community to sparkle with dancing flames. The festival falls on the day before the new moon in the month of Ashwin (October/November). Communities spare nothing in celebration. Lavish spreads of sweets and treats reflect unfettered partying. Diwali lehyam— a potent concoction made with ginger, pepper, ghee and more—is provided to help gourmands digest the sumptuous feast. Families reach out to each other with gifts of sweets, dried fruit and crunchy, salty treats. Everyone wears colorful new clothing and many even

SOUMYA SITARAMAN

new jewelry. Girls and women decorate their hands with henna designs.

What does lamp-lighting signify?

In Hindu culture, light is a powerful metaphor for knowledge and consciousness. It is a reminder of the preciousness of education, self-inquiry and improvement, which bring harmony to the individual, the community and between communities. By honoring light, we affirm the fact that from knowing arises respect for and acceptance of others. Lighting lamps reminds Hindus to keep on the right path, to dispel darkness from their hearts and minds, and to embrace knowledge and goodness.

What legends are associated with Diwali?

In the sacred text *Ramayana,* Diwali marks the return of Rama to his kingdom after defeating Ravana, the demon

Indian Carrot Sweet

Carrot Halwa
Preparation time: 20 minutes
Cooking time: 60 minutes
Serves: 6-8
Equipment: A small wok or round-bottomed pan, a ladle and a serving dish.

Ingredients
4 cups/1 kg grated carrots, 1 cup sugar, 2½ cups milk, 1½ ladles
ghee, a few cashews and raisins,
2 cardamom pods

Method
1. Wash, peel and grate the carrots.
2. Fry the cashews, raisins and cardamom in ghee and set aside.
3. Heat a ladle of ghee in the pan. Add the grated carrots and sauté.
4. Add enough milk to soak the carrots and cook on low heat, stirring occasionally, until carrots are soft. Keep adding milk, a ladle at a time, and cook until the milk thickens, then stir in the sugar.
5. Cook over low heat until everything blends together into a firm mass that separates from the sides of the pan.
6. Garnish with the fried cashews, cardamom and raisins. Top with a little ghee and pistachio slivers for extra flavor.

king who ruled Sri Lanka and kidnapped Rama's pious wife, Sita. It also celebrates Krishna's victory over Narakasura, the demon of ignorance. Rama and Krishna are earthly incarnations, or avatars, of Vishnu.

Does ritual bathing play a part?
Diwali marks the conquest of negative forces. To wipe away all traces of life's struggle, the negative and draining energies of strife, Hindus invoke the waters of India's holiest rivers—Ganga, Yamuna, Godavari, Sarasvati, Narmada, Indus and Kaveri—into water

collected in urns in preparation for an ablution after an oil massage. The special bath cleanses the physical and auric energies of the individual. Fragrant powders of dried lentils, roots, aromatic seeds, leaves and flowers are used to remove the oil. Families then don fine new clothes, beautiful patterns are drawn on the ground, and lamps are lit until entire streets glow. Even the White House in Washington, D.C., is illumined by the gentle glow of oil lamps during its annual Diwali observances.

Tidbits About Diwali

What else is done for Diwali? *Melas*, or fairs, are held in all Indian towns and villages. In the countryside, the *mela* includes a festive marketplace where farmers bring their produce to sell and clothing vendors have a heyday.

What are the giant effigies that are burned by big crowds? Huge effigies of Ravana, with ten heads, are built of straw and filled with firecrackers. They are burned as a joyous, symbolic cleansing from evil, and lights are lit in every home, just as residents of Ayodhya did to welcome home their victorious king, Rama.

Are there customs for the day after Diwali? The following day, families offer special prayers to Lakshmi for a prosperous year. This ritual worship is also directed to Kubera,

the celestial being who distributes wealth to mortals. As Hindus pray for comfort and the family's material wealth, it is believed that things should not be given away or donated on this one day of the year.

Hinduism: Fact & Fiction

FACT: Believing that the Divine resides in all things, Hindus practice non-injury and hold a deep respect, bordering on reverence, for all living beings. This embracing attitude is reflected in India's history of welcoming refugees from all cultures and faiths. By following dharma, Hindus eschew violence and terror. Secure in their faith, they interact harmoniously with their neighbors, regardless of religious affiliation.

FICTION: Many people wrongly believe that Hindus, being proud of their religion, may disdain other cultures. In fact, Hindus fully accept the spiritual efficacy of other paths and never proselytize.

Mahasivaratri
Siva's Great Night

Mahasivaratri is the most important festival dedicated to Lord Siva. This holy day is observed by millions of Hindus all over the world. It is one of Hinduism's most esoteric holy days, when yoga practices, mantras and meditation take the devotee closer to God's essence within the core of himself. Hindus typically fast, maintain silence and stay up all night to perform spiritual practices, such as worshiping, chanting and singing. In some regions, devotees visit as many Siva temples as they can on this night.

Who is Siva?

For hundreds of millions of Hindus Siva is the Supreme Being, the absolute One God who both transcends creation and pervades it—thus existing as our own innermost essence. Siva is the powerful Deity whose energetic dance creates, sustains and dissolves the universe in endless cycles. He is the master yogi delving into unfathomable mysteries, the supreme ascetic, the prime mystic, the Light behind all light, the Life within all life. Siva is often called Mahadeva, "Great Being of Light," for He created other, lesser Gods such as Ganesha and Karttikeya. Although Siva is usually depicted as male, in reality God and the Gods are beyond gender and form, as depicted by His half-male, half-female form, Ardhanarishvara. Parvati, regarded as Siva's consort in village Hinduism,

is mystically understood as His manifest energy, inseparable from Him. The ancient *Tirumantiram* scripture says of Siva, "Himself creates. Himself preserves. Himself destroys. Himself conceals. Himself all of this He does and then grants liberation—Himself the all-pervading Lord."

What happens on Mahasivaratri?

Many Hindus perform an all-night vigil, plunging the soul into its own essence, led by Siva, the supreme yogi, who is both the guide and the goal of the search. Staying awake through the night is a sacrifice and a break from life's normal routine, a time out of time to be with God within, to reach for the realization of our true, immortal Self. Siva is known as Abhisheka Priya, "He who loves sacred ablutions," and thus many temples and home shrines have water always dripping on the Sivalinga. On this special night, Sivalingas are bathed with special substances, sometimes several times. Mahasivaratri occurs on the night before the new moon in February/March.

What is the Sivalinga?

Linga means "mark, token or sign." A Sivalinga, representing Siva, is found in virtually all of His temples. The Sivalinga is the simplest and most ancient symbol

HINDUISM TODAY

Fasting & Silence

While virtually every Hindu festival comes with a sumptuous list of foods to feast on, during Mahasivaratri most Hindus fast. A spiritual practice found in almost all of the world's religions, fasting calms the physical, mental and emotional energies, helping the devotee draw nearer to the ineffable Self within. While the most strict fast on nothing but water; others permit themselves fruits, milk or rice.

Many observe silence on this night, thinking of nothing but God. Silence, known in Sanskrit as mauna, quiets the demands of the mind and body, bringing forth spiritual clarity.

In Hinduism, God is not separate from creation. A virtuous life and certain techniques, such as yoga and ascetic practices, allow a person to remove the veil that makes us think of ourselves as separate from Him.

of the Divine. It is especially evocative of Parasiva, God beyond all forms and qualities, the unmanifested Absolute. Sivalingas are commonly made of stone, but may also be of metal, precious gems, crystal, wood, earth or even transitory materials like sand or ice. Ardent devotees make special Sivalingas to worship during Mahasivaratri.

Is there a special mantra for Siva?
Namah Sivaya is among the foremost Vedic mantras. It means "adoration to Siva" and is called the Panchakshara, or "five-letters." The five elements, too, are embodied in this ancient formula for invocation. Na is earth, Ma is water, Si is fire, Va is air, and Ya is ether, or space.

Tidbits About Mahasivaratri

What is holy ash? Holy ash is a sacrament that is dear to devotees of Siva. Taken from sacred fires, it purifies and blesses those who wear it. This fine, white powder is worn on the forehead as a reminder of the temporary nature of the physical body and the urgency to strive for spiritual attainment and closeness to God.

What is the special offering to Siva? Hindus believe that offering bilva leaves (*Aegle marmelos*) on Mahasivaratri is most auspicious. Legend tells of a hunter who was chased by a tiger. Scrambling up a thorny tree, he plucked and dropped its leaves to stay alert. The tree was a bilva, The leaves happened to fall on a Sivalinga, and it was the night of Sivaratri. That all-night worship of God, though inadvertent, earned the hunter liberation from rebirth.

Siva accepts devotees irrespective of their faults and foibles, forgiving man's cognizant and innocent mistakes.

What is the Kumbha Mela? The Kumbha Mela is a grand festival held every few years in rotation at four places where several sacred rivers converge: Haridwar, Prayag, Nasik and Ujjain. The largest melas, at Haridwar and Prayag, fall in January to April and often include Mahasivaratri. Devotees come from near and far to immerse themselves in the holy waters, with prayers for purification and spiritual liberation on their lips. In 2001, the Kumbha Mela at Prayag, held on the river bank, was attended by more than 60 million people. It was the biggest human gathering held on Earth, seven times the population of New York City.

Fact & Fiction

FACT: Hindus undergo numerous traditional rites of passage at critical junctures throughout life. These ceremonies invoke divine blessings for the individual and help bind him with his community as he advances on the path of virtue. Name-giving, first feeding, commencement of learning, coming of age, marriage and cremation are primary examples. **FICTION:** It is commonly believed that rituals are mandatory. In fact, there are no absolute requirements within Hinduism. Each devotee is free to practice his faith according to his family tradition and personal preferences.

WWW.DINODIA.COM

Holi
Splashed with Colors of Friendship

Holi is wild and raucous, a frolic of friendly playfulness. During Holi, India's streets are overtaken by crowds awash with colored powder. Not only clothes, but faces, arms and hair are smeared and sprayed with every color of the rainbow. People sing, dance, play, hug each other and smile with such child-like joy that it makes one wonder where so much happiness comes from! No religious festival in the world compares to Holi in terms of engaging young and old alike. It is a celebration of love, forgiveness, hope and just plain fun.

SHUTTERSTOCK

What is Holi?

Holi is a community's exuberant expression of joy to welcome the warmth of spring. In a reflection of nature's abundance, Hindus celebrate with bursts of color, camaraderie and shared abandon. It begins on Purnima, full moon day, in the Hindu month of Phalguni (February/March) and lasts for as long as 16 days.

How does the festival start?

Many communities create a central bonfire on the night before Holi, starting with kindling and logs and adding organic debris as they clean up their property. The fire symbolizes the torching of negative or troublesome experiences and memories. An effigy of Holika, a demoness personifying negativity, is consigned to the flames, and freshly harvested barley and oats are offered. The embers are collected to light sacred fires, and the ashes are used to mark the forehead as a blessing.

When does the color fun begin?

On the day of Holi, people celebrate by playing, dancing and running in the streets. Water pistols are filled with colored water and squirted on family, friends and strangers alike. Dye powders and water balloons are a big part of the play. The wise wear old clothes, usually white, in anticipation of the mess! Virtually anything goes, including humor, practical jokes and teasing—all excused with the saying, "Don't mind, it's Holi!" (Hindi: *Bura na mano, Holi hai.*) Men are at the playful mercy of women, who dance with them. Especially in North India, people celebrate with abandon, even splashing color on their homes as a prelude to the more sober custom of renewing the paint with shell-based white. Deities and images of ancestors are hand-painted and placed in beautiful altars. Dramatic events feature devotional songs and the retelling of the love epic of Radha and Krishna. Bonds are renewed, particularly among in-laws and the extended family. Etiquette on Holi requires that one accept all overtures with an open heart, burying grievances to begin relationships afresh. People of all walks of life mingle and greet, applying vermilion on each other's foreheads in an uninhibited exchange of goodwill.

What are the delicacies of this festival?

Special sweet and savory treats including *mathri, puran poli* and *vadai* are made. Many communities make an intoxicating, cooling drink, called *thandai*, made of purified water, sugar, seeds of watermelon, muskmelon and lotus, along with nuts, cardamom, fennel, white pepper, saffron and rose petals.

WWW.DINODIA.COM

Making Safe, Natural Colors

Dyes made of toxic chemicals are too often used during Holi. The food-based recipes below, along with edible food coloring, offer safe alternatives for all colors.

RED: Soak red pomegranate rind in water overnight. A pinch of edible gypsum mixed with turmeric powder in water gives a bright red. Soak red hibiscus flowers in water overnight.

YELLOW: Turmeric powder makes a terrific yellow.

BROWN: Soak betel nut in water overnight and dilute as necessary. Or boil tea or coffee in water.

PURPLE: Boil blueberries in an iron vessel and let stand overnight.

MAGENTA: Slice or grate one beet root. Leave overnight in water. Dilute as needed for different shades.

GREEN: Purée spinach, coriander or mint leaves in water. Strain and use.

Tidbits About Holi

What is the meaning behind the bonfire? Love, positive values and goodness are celebrated on Holi. Their triumphs over divisiveness and negative forces have been reinforced in legends, such as that of Holika and her brother Prahlad. The famous king Hiranyakashipu had earned a boon that made him virtually indestructible. Blinded by this power, he thought he was God, the only being worthy of worship. His young son Prahlad was devoted to Lord Vishnu and refused to obey his father. Infuriated, the king devised the cruelest punishments. In one attempt, Prahlad's evil aunt Holika, who possessed the power to withstand fire, tricked him into climbing a burning pyre with her. Prahlad's love for true Divinity protected him from the flames. Holika burned while Prahlad lived. The bonfire of Holi is symbolic of this victory of good over evil.

How did the frolicking with color originate? Legend has it that Krishna noticed one day how much lighter Radha's complexion was than His own. His mother playfully suggested that He smear Radha's cheeks with color to make Her look like Him, which Krishna did. The strong-willed Radha gleefully retaliated, and a merry chaos ensued. Another legend has it that Krishna celebrated this festival with His friends and the gopis. They danced and frolicked, filling the air with color in a joyous welcome of spring.

Is this a romantic occasion? The festive dancing and camaraderie create the perfect environment for matrimonial alliances. Young people find mates, and families formally seal marital agreements during these days.

WWW.DINODIA.COM

Fact & Fiction

FACT: Hindus worship and celebrate the Divine with unparalleled variety and fervor. Dance, song, prayer, meditation, processions, pilgrimage, bathing, painting, symbols and rituals are all valid ways of connecting with Divinity. This is living testimony to the existence of many paths within this ancient faith, all leading to God. Each person finds his own path among the many laid out by gurus and sages. To the Hindu, spiritual life is meant to be lived joyously, as Holi demonstrates.

FICTION: Hinduism is rich with stories of the Gods and their wives. Yet, on a deeper, philosophical level, it is widely regarded as a fiction that the Gods are married. The Supreme Being and the Gods are neither male nor female and are therefore not married.

Maps

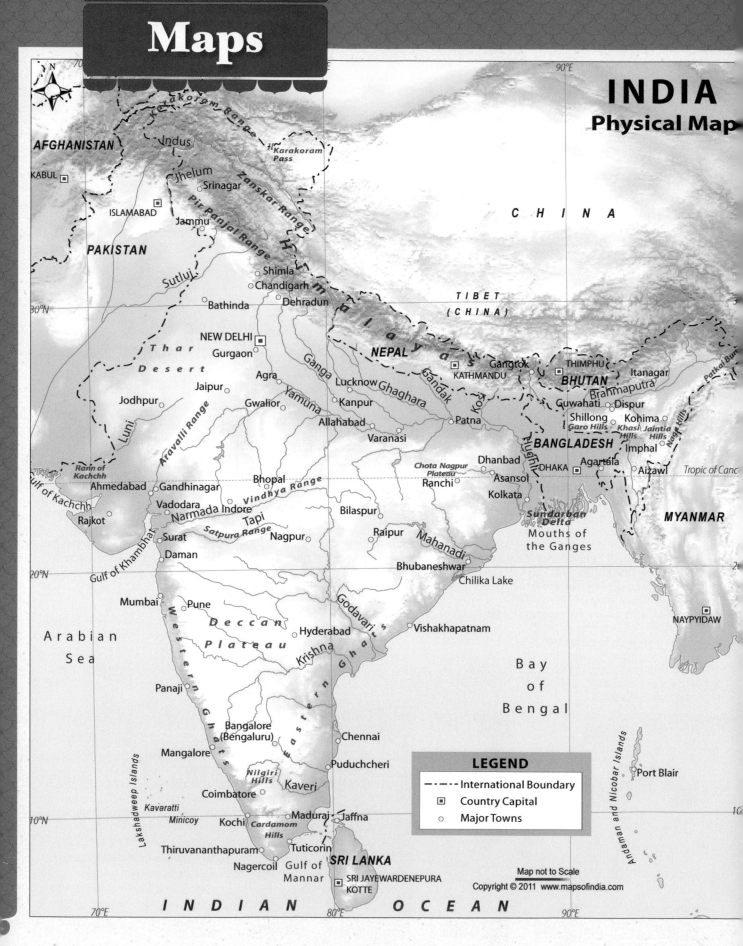

INDIA
Physical Map

N

AFGHANISTAN

KABUL

Karakoram Range
Indus
Karakoram Pass

ISLAMABAD

Jhelum
Srinagar
Zanskar Range
Jammu
Pir Panjal Range

PAKISTAN

Sutlej

Shimla
Chandigarh
Dehradun

Bathinda

Thar Desert

NEW DELHI
Gurgaon

Agra
Jaipur

Jodhpur

Aravalli Range

Ganga
Lucknow Ghaghara
Kanpur
Yamuna
Gwalior
Allahabad
Varanasi

C H I N A

TIBET
(CHINA)

NEPAL

KATHMANDU

Gandak

Kosi

Gangtok
THIMPHU
BHUTAN
Itanagar

Brahmaputra
Guwahati Dispur
Shillong Kohima
Garo Hills Khasi Jaintia
Hills Hills
Imphal

Patna

Naga Hills
Patkai Bum

Luni

Rann of
Kachchh

Ahmedabad
Gandhinagar
Vadodara Indore
Narmada
Bhopal
Vindhya Range

Chota Nagpur
Plateau
Ranchi

Dhanbad
Asansol

Hugli
DHAKA
BANGLADESH
Agartala
Aizawl

Tropic of Canc

Gulf of Kachchh

Rajkot

Tapi
Satpura Range
Surat
Daman

Bilaspur
Nagpur

Raipur
Mahanadi

Kolkata

Sundarban
Delta

MYANMAR

Mouths of
the Ganges

Arabian
Sea

Gulf of Khambhat

Mumbai Pune

Deccan
Plateau

Godavari

Hyderabad

Krishna

Bhubaneshwar
Chilika Lake

Vishakhapatnam

B a y
o f
B e n g a l

NAYPYIDAW

Western Ghats

Eastern Ghats

Panaji

Bangalore
(Bengaluru)
Mangalore

Chennai

Nilgiri
Hills
Kaveri
Coimbatore

Puduchcheri

Lakshadweep Islands

Kavaratti
Minicoy

Kochi
Thiruvananthapuram
Nagercoil

Madurai Jaffna
Cardamom
Hills

Tuticorin
Gulf of
Mannar

SRI LANKA

SRI JAYEWARDENEPURA
KOTTE

Andaman and Nicobar Islands

Port Blair

LEGEND
–·–·– International Boundary
▣ Country Capital
○ Major Towns

Map not to Scale
Copyright © 2011 www.mapsofindia.com

I N D I A N   O C E A N

70°E   80°E   90°E

30°N
20°N
10°N

70°E   90°E

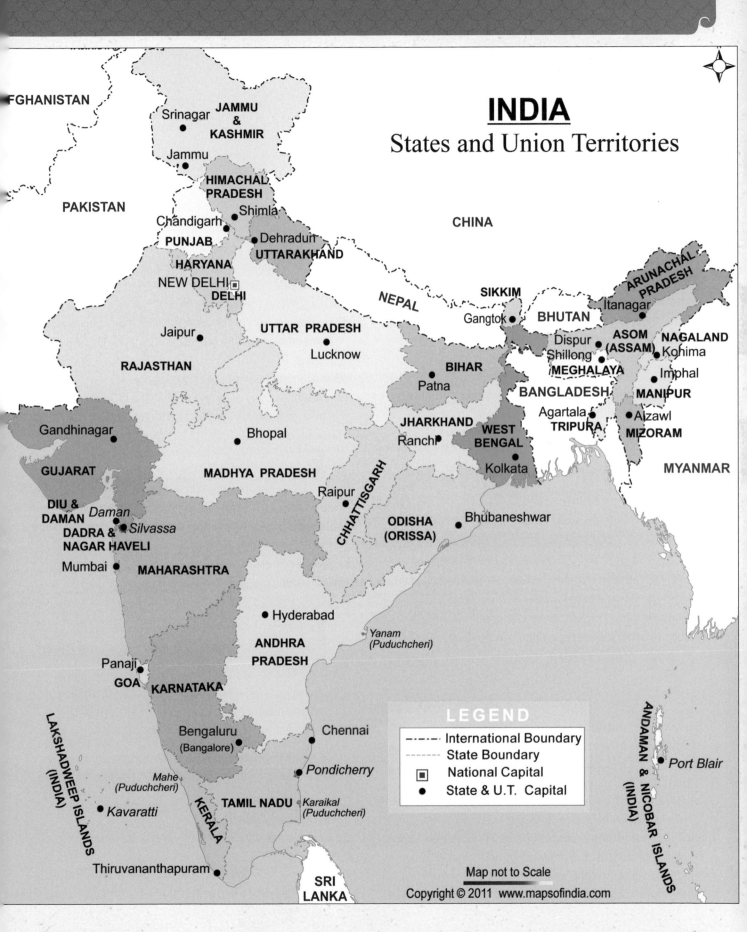

INDIA
States and Union Territories

AFGHANISTAN

PAKISTAN

CHINA

NEPAL

BHUTAN

BANGLADESH

MYANMAR

SRI LANKA

JAMMU & KASHMIR
Srinagar
Jammu

HIMACHAL PRADESH
Shimla

Chandigarh
PUNJAB

Dehradun
UTTARAKHAND

HARYANA

NEW DELHI
DELHI

Jaipur

RAJASTHAN

UTTAR PRADESH
Lucknow

SIKKIM
Gangtok

ARUNACHAL PRADESH
Itanagar

Dispur
ASOM (ASSAM)
Shillong
MEGHALAYA

NAGALAND
Kohima

Imphal
MANIPUR

BIHAR
Patna

Agartala
TRIPURA

Aizawl
MIZORAM

Gandhinagar

GUJARAT

DIU & DAMAN
Daman
DADRA & NAGAR HAVELI
Silvassa

Mumbai
MAHARASHTRA

Bhopal
MADHYA PRADESH

CHHATTISGARH
Raipur

JHARKHAND
Ranchi

WEST BENGAL
Kolkata

ODISHA (ORISSA)
Bhubaneshwar

Hyderabad

ANDHRA PRADESH

Yanam (Puduchcheri)

Panaji
GOA
KARNATAKA

Bengaluru
(Bangalore)

Chennai

Pondicherry

Mahe (Puduchcheri)

LAKSHADWEEP ISLANDS (INDIA)
Kavaratti

KERALA

TAMIL NADU
Karaikal (Puduchcheri)

Thiruvananthapuram

ANDAMAN & NICOBAR ISLANDS (INDIA)
Port Blair

LEGEND
-·-·- International Boundary
- - - State Boundary
☐ National Capital
● State & U.T. Capital

Map not to Scale

Copyright © 2011 www.mapsofindia.com

Glossary

A

Advaita Vedanta: a non-dualist philosophy taught by Adi Shankara (p. 34)

Agamas: Hindu scriptures explaining philosophy, personal conduct, worship and temple construction (p. 9)

ahimsa: nonviolence (p. 8)

Alvars: Vaishnavite saints of the Bhakti Movement (p. 33)

annex: to add a conquered country to one's own (p. 43)

arati: waving of an oil lamp in front of the Deity during worship (p. 13)

ashram: a Hindu spiritual community (p. 75)

ashtanga yoga: "eight-limbed yoga," a Hindu spiritual practice which includes hatha yoga (p. 92)

atman: God within man (p. 7)

austerity: difficult practice of self-denial and discipline (p. 12)

ayurveda: ancient Indian medical system (p. 29)

B

bhajana: call-and-response devotional singing (p. 52)

Bhakti Movement: popular devotional movement within Hindusm, started around the fifth century ce (p. 33)

Bharatanatyam: ancient temple dance of India (p. 55)

British Raj: the government of India from 1858 to 1947 (p. 64)

C

Carnatic: classical music system of India (p. 53)

Central Government: the national government of India (p. 84)

chakra: a center of energy and consciousness in the spiritual body (p. 94)

colonize: to take control of another country and settle it with immigrants from one's own (p. 62)

colonized mind: the feeling of inferiority which persists in a colonized people long after independence (p. 69–71)

consciousness: thought, awareness, perception (p. 94)

conversion: to change one's religion (p. 47)

cremation: to dispose of a dead body by burning it (p. 74)

D

Dalits: lowest caste of Hindus, also "Untouchables" (p. 49)

Deity: the Supreme God or a God (p. 8)

deva: a divine being (p. 7)

Devi: a name of the Goddess (p. 33)

dharma: a key Hindu concept which includes the ideas of righteousness, divine law, ethics, religion, duty, justice and truth (p. 8)

diksha: an initiation or rite of passage (p. 72)

Dravidian: a family of languages spoken in South India and Sri Lanka, or the people who speak them (p. 4)

E

ecstasy: feeling or expressing overwhelming joy in God (p. 47)

egalitarian: the principle that all people deserve equal rights and opportunities (p. 68)

empire: a group of countries under a single ruler (p. 65)

ethics: moral principles that govern behavior (p. 8)

F

famine: extreme scarcity of food (p. 42)

Freethought: a movement strong in the 1900s valuing science, logic and reason over authority or tradition (p. 91)

G

Ganesha: Hindu God who is Lord of Obstacles, recognizable by His elephant head (p. 7)

God: the Supreme God, transcendent and immanent; or one of the Gods (p. 6)

Goddess: the Supreme God when regarded as feminine; or one of the female Deities (p. 6)

Gods: when plural, one of the divine beings created by the Supreme Being (p. 7)

guru: "one who removes darkness," a teacher (p. 14)

H

Hindi: fourth most spoken language in the world; related to ancient Sanskrit (p. 23)

Hinduism: the majority religion of India, followed by 1.1 billion people worldwide; called Sanatana Dharma, "eternal religion," in Sanskrit (p. 32)

holistic: based on the idea that the parts of a whole are interconnected (p. 92)

I

immanent: present everywhere and in all things (p. 7)

imperial: of or relating to an empire (p. 23)

initiation: a ceremony given by a priest, teacher or guru to bring a person into a new level of education, religious practice and spiritual awareness (p. 72–74)

Inquisition: a movement within the Catholic Church to identify and punish heretics (p. 46)

J

Jainism: a religion founded in India in the 6th century bce by Mahavira (p. 32)

japa: repetition of a sacred sound, such as "Aum" (p. 75)

jati: a community or tribe in India usually holding a particular occupation (p. 4)

jizya: a tax on non-Muslim citizens of an Islamic state (p. 44)

K

kafir: in Islam, a term for a non-believer 48)

karma: the law of cause and effect (p. 8)

kirtana: call-and-response devotional singing (p. 52)

Krishna: one of Lord Vishnu's ten avatars, or appearances upon Earth as a divine personality (p. 7)

L

Lakshmi: Goddess of wealth (p.15)

M

mantra: a sacred word or phrase, usually in Sanskrit (p. 74)

meditation: practice of quieting the mind to enter a higher state of awareness (p. 92)

mela: a large gathering of people; a fair (p. 15)

mendicant: a holy person who lives by begging (p. 14)

metaphysics: the inner study of reality beyond the five senses (p. 94)

missionary: a person of one religion sent to convert people of another religion (p. 49)

monk: a male member of a religious community under vows (p. 75)

mudra: a hand gesture with a specific meaning (p. 55)

murti: Sanskrit term for the consecrated statue in a Hindu temple; best translated as "Deity" in English (p. 8)

mystical: concerned with the soul or spirit, rather than material things (p. 49)

N

nadaswaram: a high pitched, double-reed wooden horn (p. 31)

nadi: in yoga, an energy channel within the body (p. 94)

namaste: "I bow to you;" traditional Hindu greeting usually said with the hands pressed together (p. 2)

Nataraja: "King of Dance;" a form of Lord Siva (p. 21)

nationalism: patriotic feelings, principles or efforts (p. 62)

New Age: a Western spiritual movement drawing on Eastern thought (p. 91)

P

paddy: unhusked rice (p. 31)

panchayat: a village council (p. 29)

Partition: the division of British India into modern India and Pakistan (p. 65)

patriot: a person who vigorously supports their country and is prepared to defend it (p. 62)

polytheist: one who believes in or worships more than one God (p. 48)

puja: a ceremony to invoke God with the ringing of bells, passing of flames, chanting, and presentation of flowers, incense and other offerings (p. 7)

Puranas: Hindu scriptures with stories of God and the Gods as well as spiritual teachings, historical traditions, geography and culture (p. 9)

R

raga: a pattern of notes used in musical composition (p. 53)

reincarnation: rebirth of the soul in a new body (p. 8)

reservations: In modern India, a program of affirmative action for disadvantaged groups (p. 86)

rites of passage: social and religious ceremonies marking important stages in a person's life (p. 72)

S

salvation: in Western religions, the belief one is "saved" by God from the effect of sin and allowed into a divine afterlife; similar to Hindu idea of moksha, or release from rebirth (p. 6)

samskara: a rite of passage, such as name-giving or first feeding (p. 12)

Sanatana Dharma: "Eternal Truth," the ancient name for what is now called the Hindu religion (p. 6)

sannyasin: a Hindu monk (p. 75)

Sanskrit: the ancient and sacred language of India (p. 3)

satyagraha: "truth force," Gandhi's method of passive political resistance (p. 65)

sepoy: an Indian soldier in the British army (p. 44)

Shakta: a denomination of Hinduism worshiping the female aspect of God (p. 7)

Shakti: name of God in feminine form (p. 15)

shastra: Hindu legal texts written in Sanskrit (p. 25)

Sikh: a religion of India founded by Guru Nanak in the 15th century (p. 47)

sindur: a red powder traditionally worn by married women in the part of their hair (p. 74)

Siva: the Supreme God (p. 2)

Smarta: a major denomination of Hinduism (p. 7)

sthree dhana: "woman's wealth;" jewelry or other valuables

brought to a marriage by the bride (p. 72)

Surya Namaskara: "greetings to the Sun;" a series of hatha yoga poses (p. 93)

swami: a Hindu monk (p. 14)

T

tala: a rhythmic pattern in Indian music systems (p. 53)

theology: the systematic study of the nature of God and religious belief (p. 91)

tolerance: willingness to allow beliefs, opinions or behavior that one does not necessarily agree with (p. 32)

transcendent: existing beyond the physical universe, said of God (p. 6)

Transcendentalist: an idealistic philosophy teaching that Divinity pervades all of nature and humanity (p. 91)

U

Upanishads: Hindu scriptures that are part of the *Vedas;* mostly about philosophy (p. 91)

V

Vaishnava: a major denomination of Hinduism (p. 7)

varna: a division of society into four broad classes—priests, warriors, merchants and workers (p. 4)

Vastu: Hindu architecture and town planning (p. 34)

Veda: sacred texts of Hinduism (p. 3)

Vedanta: a Hindu philosophy based on the *Upanishads* (p. 34)

Vishnu: the Supreme God in the Vaishnavite tradition (p. 7)

W

worldly: of or concerned with material values or ordinary life rather than a spiritual existence (p. 75)

Y

yajna: Hindu fire ceremony (p. 3)

Index